The Waterlily

A Blue Mountains Journal

KATE LLEWELLYN

The Waterlily

A Blue Mountains Journal

HUDSON

HAWTHORN

Hudson Publishing
(A division of N.S. Hudson Publishing Services Pty Ltd)
6 Muir Street, Hawthorn, Victoria 3122

Copyright © Kate Llewellyn 1987
First published 1987
Reprinted 1987
First published in paperback 1988
Reprinted 1989

LaserSet by N.S. Hudson Publishing Services Pty Ltd
Printed in Australia by
Australian Print Group, Maryborough, Victoria
Cover design by Nick Hudson
Cover photograph by Ken Stepnell

Australian C.I.P. data

Llewellyn, Kate, 1940-
  The waterlily : a Blue Mountains journal.

  ISBN 0 949873 16 0.

  1. Llewellyn, Kate, 1940- -Diaries. 2. Women poets,
  Australian - Diaries. I. Title.

A821'.3

Contents

Acknowledgements

The author and publishers would like to thank Judith Rodriguez for permission to reproduce her poem, 'How do you know its the right one?' from *Witch Heart* (Sisters Publishing, Melbourne, 1982), distributed by Murphy Sisters, 240 The Parade, Norwood, SA, 5067.

To Jerry Rogers
with gratitude

~ 1 ~

September

When I came to live in the mountains I was determined to be happy. Sparrows were pecking the pale green and white shoots from the tree outside the kitchen as I made the first cup of tea for the day. I looked at them, watching them puff up their feathers and decided to write a journal. It's three months since I bought this house and now I am making a garden. I read Edna Walling daily and long to talk to her. She's dead so I can't. I've planted fifty-six different varieties of plants and walk out in my dressing-gown with a cup of tea each morning to see how they have coped overnight. Just like Matron's round.

The Australian Literary Supplement today has a contest for a short story in fifty words so I wrote one sitting in the back sunroom eating toast and bean sprouts.

In a minute I am riding Woolfie's bike up the street to have coffee at Snaps with the Denisons and to buy some pansy plants for the plot where I had the pine taken out. Lydia put a stick in the centre of it and said, 'See, there's your magnolia'. David had just draped the hose round to make a curve and I stood back on the verandah and saw that it looked right. Miss Walling would have liked it. She taught them a lot too.

My son Hugh rang to say he has the phone on now at Kirribilli and he is going to town to buy a saucepan. This is the first flat he has had alone and now that his girlfriend has left him he is becoming macho to hide the squeaking twigs inside that keep on sighing. He can't ever manage it convincingly. He sees even a football match as an intellectual even though he is trying hard to fit in. In other words, he doesn't fool me. He told D, who is coming up on the train today to stay overnight, that there's only flowers and poetry up at Kate's and he's not into that ... just football and beer. I said on the phone that if he comes up to stay again I won't talk about gardens, and if I do, it'll only be vegetables such as zucchini, cucumbers and eggplants. He laughed.

Down in my lane where I plan to plant an avenue of silver birches when I can pay for them, I have planted ratatouille ... all I need now is the olive tree for the oil to cook it. It is draped with white ribbons to scare off the birds. The ribbons are tafetta and flutter in the wind. I found them in a box left over from when my daughter rowed in Head of the River and we decorated hundreds of straw boaters with the school colours. I also put these ribbons over the new all-white garden I planted in the old rubbish dump. The white azaleas with the ribbons floating over them look like a windy funeral. I wonder if white's bad luck. I can never get enough of it.

Today I saw three white hyacinths out and debated about bringing one inside for the scent, but I didn't. It looks a bit childish the way I planted the bulbs in a row when I first came here: a big bag of daffodils, hyacinths and tulips. The seventeen roses I planted in a curving row have all survived and even doubled in size. It is said they should bloom in November. Roses for Christmas. Perhaps.

It is getting cold so I lit the fire when I came in after Snaps café. Oh, I'm dying to write so let's not beat around the bush. I planted climbing French beans and zucchini seeds today. Then three bundles of pansies and one of blue viola and a lot of petunias. Whatever day lilies are, I now have two in the plot where the pine was, along with a lot more petunias. I know few real gardeners plant annuals, they are really for amateurs, but I do love the scent of petunias on hot nights when you can sit outside drinking and their scent rises up from the lawn. Even as I plant I'm aware none of this may grow ... it's all very hit and miss with me. In the end I expect to be able to say I was good at onions as I think they are probably indestructible. I put them round the roses because I read they keep aphids away and then sprays aren't needed. That was just the excuse I needed to pop vegetables in the flower beds. Like putting boys in with girls. I'm looking for my copy of Marcus Aurelius as I think he will be just the thing to go with gardening. I haven't unpacked many books yet and the study is a great mess of old frocks spilling out of boxes. All the stuff that can neither be kept nor thrown out.

When I told David this morning that Hugh had said there

was nothing but flowers and poems here, David said to invite him back and they could have a wrestle on the back lawn and sit on the step and have spitting contests, then try to see who could pee over the shed roof and that if he wanted to he could try out David's wood splitter. I had better go and meet the train as D will be peering out of the window by now looking for the Leura stop. In the end I did pick a white hyacinth, here have a sniff.

Sunday, 29 September
I have just walked outside. The moon is full. It is sailing across the sky above a pine like a huge white coach pulled by invisible horses. There's the aura of a rainbow round it like a promise. D has gone back on the train and I am alone again. We planted a Japanese maple outside my bedroom window. She went and lay on my bed to see if where I stood holding up the spade was visible from my pillows. After walking about five feet farther on it became visible so that is where we put it. Planted like a stick of dynamite. We both heaved and grunted at the size and weight of the roots, trying not to break up the mass as the nurseryman told me to be careful; this month or so it is putting out delicate hair roots. It sounded like a labour ward and D said just as it was falling into its bed, 'A difficult birth'.

Earlier we walked to the escarpment and then to the pool of Siloam and then on to Lyrebird Dell. There is a waterfall at both these places and at Lyrebird Dell the pool is quite deep. I hope like mad I can swim there in summer. If I retreat from living here it won't be the winters that drive me out, it will be the summers.

Today I had anxieties about the last-minute poems to put in my new book. In two days it will be too late to change anything. I rang the editor and she seemed so calm I felt too foolish to tell her, although I suppose my voice told it all, that I was fast with panic. This book has had six drafts and although I have been weary of it, now I care as though I am about to have it delivered from me. It's to be called *Luxury*. Goodnight.

~ 2 ~

October

The first daffodils are out and I took some to the city. It means that up here it takes three and a half months for them to flower from the planting. I put them in the first week I came to this house. Pale blue forget-me-not grows wild here. It looks wonderful with daffodils in the basket. My Mother used to make floral carpets from blue forget-me-nots.

The making of floral carpets is, I think, a dying art. They are post-object art, although no one who made them had heard of that at the time. The heads of tiny flowers are stuck into a tray of damp sand as if they were paint and the sand canvas. They only last a day or two and take hours to make. They often smell wonderful and as you look you know they are dying. All those beautiful carpets are gone without trace. No one thought to take a photograph. I mean to ask my Mother to make one for me when I visit her next and to photograph that.

It is dry here already and so as soon as I got home I watered the garden and then put tomato dust over most things as something is eating the roses and four tomatoes have disappeared entirely. Only the little pictures of tomatoes are still there like a tombstone to say they once lived.

In Sydney I got *New American Poets of the '80's* and read it coming home. Maura Stanton is in it. She is so good and simply my favourite poet at the moment. I wrote to her once having seen her poems in the *American Poetry Review* years ago and she wrote back in her calm fashion from the University of Illinois where my letter had been sent from Utah. Quite a feat for the letter to find her, she said, but I don't know much about America. She mentioned dogwood in one of those new poems. I have a second dogwood now about to go in but it has hair roots this month and so I must keep it a few more weeks in its pot. It has large bracts of white flowers the tag says. 'Bracts' is a good word. I say it over when I see the sticks that are all that is showing at present of the first one I planted two months ago. They remind me of American literature. I think Mark Twain mentions the dogwood.

Today *Compass* magazine arrived in the post with fifty dollars inside for a story I wrote, so now I am off to buy a white magnolia. And if anyone wishes to mention the electricity bill they can hush their mouth.

Thursday, 3 October

Gordon and Woolfie are here and we went to the Hydro Majestic for a drink late this afternoon on our way to the Megalon Valley. Six white donkeys with two white foals stood in a paddock as we came round the bend. The sunset was pink on the hill and one of the foals stood against the horizon to have its photo taken. A dead white cockatoo lay on the road. I feel dead birds are bad omens. Woolfie put cherry blossom in a jug in the kitchen beside a dish of two pink camellia heads that had fallen off the plants when I went out this morning to empty the tea leaves on to them. They are the size of a saucer; I know as I measured one.

Friday, 4 October

The first tulip is out today. It is red with a black heart like a Norse helmsman. If it were a person it would be called Eric. Pale blue pansies are flapping in the breeze. I walked down my lane with the wheelbarrow and dug a load of old oak leaves and lugged the barrow up like an ant struggling with a crumb. It's round the roses and poppies now as the highest part of the side garden is dry and eroded. In a Mosman street dump I picked up a piece of wire netting before I came here and said it would be for the first sweetpeas. But I used it today to help the two clematis I planted at the back steps. One is a lilac-blue colour, the label says. The other had no label. I hope it is pink or white. Yesterday I dragged some old galvanised iron sheets over to prop up the fence and to keep the dogs out, I hope. All day I wore a sundress and was grumpy. I don't know why.

Gordon and Woolfie left this morning so it is very quiet except for a Mozart concerto on the radio. They dropped me off in the main street and I walked home with the shopping among trees of white blossom. I think they are white cherry. I plan to get some to put on the lawn outside in the street. The front door had the first coat of cream paint on yesterday and although it is a lot better than the red it was, it is a great mess. I am not sure all the stripping of paint I did, which gave me such a headache days later, was any use. My plan is to pile on the gloss until it is so thick all faults will disappear.

There is a snake's nest down the lane. As I pulled up an old piece of iron for the fence I saw it. I think many a small bird has disappeared down that hole and never been seen again. There is a pickled snake in a jar along with a goanna and a bat in the same condition. I found them when I had the shed pulled down. They are in the toolshed now (a euphemism for the old outdoor lavatory where I keep these things to show children). I daren't really look at them but pass them out with eyes averted. They are truly hell's curiosities.

Today I am expecting beans. I have been down looking at where they were put in but so far see only weeds that most weirdly mimic them. Perhaps tomorrow.

Sunday, 6 October
Today I walked home with Lydia and David under the vast flowering pink cherry trees in the Mall. Lydia said their name but I forget it. They have burgundy leaves. Standing under them, David is so tall – seven feet or just less. He looked as if he was wearing a gigantic pink hat, as if he was Lady Bracknell or perhaps off to heaven's best party. (You see how these excesses of nature make anyone excessive.)

I put soil from an old pot plant over the oak leaves on the poor soil that I am trying to improve. The leaves were blowing away like old letters, meaningless, without destination. Like lives at times. In these amateurish ways I try to be a real gardener. As will be obvious by now I am learning about this from books and friends. The garden has a slightly raffish childish air as if some children played at making a garden one long hot day being mercifully quiet for their Mother who was indoors lying on a pink silk quilt with a headache, a lavender bag on her forehead.

It has been a very good morning. Lydia found a lilac flowering on the side of the house where the drive is. I hadn't known there was a lilac there as it is hidden by the prunus.

There is a cake in the oven for a lunch party and I have a face mask on and can barely blink. If I drink I must use a straw.

The small citrus tree I am trying to save now has dark green leaves among some yellow ones. It has had six different things put on in attempts to save it. Something must be working. I hope it is a lemon tree. Lemon with everything I say.

Saturday, 12 October
After five days in Sydney I came home yesterday to find the trees misty with green, like a veil they have been crocheting daily. Such a little time makes a difference. Four red tulips out blazing. It's easy to see why Sylvia Plath wrote her *Tulips* poem. The red is so bright, in a white hospital room after being ill it would be like a wound. She didn't much like them.

In the lane the vegetables have been sorting things out. Lettuces, surprisingly, are thriving and now three inches across yet the aubergines are limp and upset as if they skun their knees. Capsicums not keen on life either. Ten beans thrusting up. They are very sexy.

In the rain this afternoon I planted old green potatoes from a blue dish I had put them in after cutting them into pieces that are shooting. Last night I cooked some for dinner and there was a green star vein in their heart. It is difficult to buy potatoes up here at present that are not pea-green when they leave the shop. Some say they are poisonous. Yet did you ever hear of anyone ill from eating cooked green potatoes?

It is the day of the Leura Fair. Gordon, Woolfie and I walked up the closed-off street in the rain and felt wrinkled with irritation by the time we got home. I got two tall green capsicums and put them beside the tawdry ones to show them just how things might be. I don't know what might help me just now. Courage I suppose. Not really my strong point. I am planning to plant some patience and also heartsease as if they could help. Emily Dickinson was sent heartsease after a bereavement and she wrote back that she felt doubt that it might help, though the kindness was not unnoticed or unappreciated.

It is always so painful to turn away from an affair no matter how bad things have become, when to lose that person feels like cutting off a hand. Or, perhaps, leaving your house and going for a walk in a storm along the cliff alone with no coat just because you think it is the wise thing to do. I am not sure that I can do this but I know I must. A few weeks ago we planted a dogwood together and I so badly want to turn our affair into a tree.

Sunday, 13 October
What rain! The Leura Festival is washed out. David and I walked home from the shops with water dripping off our noses. My feet are cold in wet boots. I just lit the fire.

Well, I did it. In the rain I picked two red tulips and they are in a small smoked glass vase. They are howling red on the kitchen bench. Dripping with rain and scentless. Outside the dining-room window where I write this, the apple tree, as it has turned out to be, has pink-and-white blossom among the pale green leaves. The leaves are the colour of green almonds.

Yesterday, before they left for the city, Gordon and Woolfie and I watched the raising of the flag for the Festival. It was white and hung sadly like a nappy on the line from which one peg had fallen off. None of my visitors are coming as it is too wet.

Now I must enter another blasted poetry contest.

A while ago I felt so gloomy I ran out in the rain and planted a slip of white geranium in the white garden. (I got it from Peri's garden in Mosman when I stayed there last week.) Strangely, I felt better after planting it by the bird-bath. I scooped up some water with my hand and suddenly saw that lovely human gesture the priest's hand makes when he pours water on to the baby's as yet unjoined fontanelle at baptism. A daffodil had been beaten down into the mud by the rain like a fallen footballer.

Inside it is so warm now the tulips have opened. They have stamens like a black spider with a creamy yellow phallus.

Behind that is the shape like a black burnt-out memory of a daisy. Behind *that* is an aura of yellow as if the light from the fire is still glowing from embers. Weird flowers. Strange as if they fell from Mars. If they spoke, which they may any moment, it would be in Zulu.

Monday, 14 October

It has rained all night. Someone told me that the priest said yesterday, 'Lord, we draw your attention to the weather'. I laugh every time I think of it. As if God, like an elderly absent-minded gardener, cigarette dangling from a lip, was forgetfully tipping buckets on us. Nudge, nudge, 'God, give us a break will you?'

Most of the birds have disappeared with the exception of two currawongs flying silently through the mist like runners behind enemy lines. Though yesterday, as I rode my bike out to buy milk, two red king parrots were eating flat green seed-pods that had fallen on to the path. The pods looked just like green Weetbix flakes. As they dry and turn pale brown, it looks as if an angry grocer hurled his old stock into the street, furious because we wouldn't buy.

Tuesday, 15 October

Now floods. Not here; I guess the mountains won't flood till the plains are just a memory. But the Hawkesbury and Nepean rivers are in flood. Mist was swimming round the house like an opium dream when I woke up to the silence of the rain stopping. Fourteen beans are up. I keep wanting them to match the date like some lucky omen but they don't keep up. The pansies are crumpled like wet party hats.

Well, I'm puffing ... I've been planting honesty. I remarked to Lydia recently that I'd love some honesty. She silently broke off a branch of it from her garden and handed it to me. It's now along the side behind roses and will, I hope, make a pale pure backdrop to the garden. It's the most peculiar pod; inside what is very like a communion wafer rest two brown kidney-shaped seeds like twins sharing a womb. When the seeds have gone from the plant, all that remains (rather like lies when truth goes out) are empty rings like those children use to make bubbles in their baths.

Wednesday, 16 October

I have been out squashing aphids and snails. There are only a couple of capsicums left so I put a snail's remains beside the remnant of each plant in a fit of useless revenge. Gardening is violent; there is no way around it. Poisons may be quieter but they have the same effect.

The white dogwood has pale green flowers breaking out like small hands. They will turn white soon and become clusters of feathers. As you will realise, it has stopped raining, the sun is out, and my mood not improved. From fences when I went for a walk earlier, I picked lilac and white clematis and also cream freesias, blue forget-me-nots and blue scillas. They are in a pink bowl in the bathroom by the mirror, doubled in size and depth by their image. Somewhere on someone's farm walking down a warm cement path I smelt those freesias for the first time when I was about seven. I am seven now when I walk into the bathroom. I was wearing a pale green-smocked voile frock. The smocking was in pale colours, so beautiful you could drink them like milkshakes or sunsets. It had pants to match. My Mother made the frock. She had left me alone staying on the farm with her friends. I did not like them a scrap but was too afraid to ask to go home. It was my first taste of homesickness and felt like a fever of the heart. Later I was to recognise that feeling when a lover went off with someone else.

I've decided to dig up the mess of cotoneaster and agapanthus using the method of a woman called Mrs Hook who lived in our town and had three daughters whom, my Mother thought, she treated harshly. Mrs Hook once said to me, 'When one of my girls is in a bad mood, I set her to work on the kitchen floor. She takes it out on that'. I was struck at once by how unsympathetic she was to those daughters. Something so cold and utilitarian. Why not get the happiest one to wash it? The atmosphere would be more pleasant. Punishment for unhappiness seemed to me to be doubly unkind. My Mother had a passing respect for Mrs Hook, though she didn't really like her. When my Father died, Mr Hook arrived with a tree in his car and planted it in the garden for, as he said, 'Brink's memory'. Then he drove away.

Later

Well, that didn't work, because someone had tipped a load of rocks and woodchips on the front garden in an attempt to keep out weeds. It's impossible to dig.

Suddenly, out of the blue ... bees. Bees in the apple blossom, blowflies in the kitchen. The sound of a blowfly to most Australians anywhere on earth is the sound of summer. Bzzzzzzz ... summer. I lay in the sun and read C.W.Lewis. He said something that makes me laugh every time I think of it: 'horrible nations have horrible religions.' I don't suppose the horrible nation thinks it's horrid nor that its religion is that bad either. Some cannibals might find they have a lot in common with Christianity.

I planted some pumpkin seeds from the piece I ate for lunch today. Every time I plant something I think of Peter Rabbit and Mr McGregor on hands and knees planting out young cabbages. Then I think of Beatrix Potter herself and how she unwittingly gave me some of the best advice I ever had. In her biography it is said that she used the Bible when she felt her writing was getting flat. She would go off and read a part of the Bible, not I am certain the new version, but the old. (The alteration of the Bible is one of the greatest pieces of literary vandalism of this century.) She found her own writing immediately improved. It is a good trick – any piece of good writing will do, it need not be the Bible. It doesn't mean at all that you write in the same style after reading for this purpose, but that your writing improves. Try it if you like.

Thursday, 17 October

Last night a terrific electric storm. Lights failed. I took a bath with candles burning by the bathroom mirror and the lightning turning the garden an eerie whitish-blue. I lay up to my neck in hot water staring out of the window and then saw a huge black spider creeping across the ceiling. Just for the effect. Gothic movies are made like this. Grasping my nerve, a towel and a candle I climbed into bed hoping to sleep with courage warm beside me.

Sunlight and cheerful blue sky this morning until the weather changed again. Now I must go to the city, wangle my way out of this difficult affair, if I can, and retreat with as many of my troops as I can save. Wish me luck. Perhaps I should call this journal 'Memoirs of a Drama Queen'.

Monday, 20 October
Home to behind the lines. Now a waterlily has appeared in the front yard. Was it an omen? Standing by the pond, the man I went to the city to see said in his usual laconic manner, 'You have a waterlily coming'. There it was, half-hidden by ivy, with two leaves floating just for frogs in fairy tales to sit on recounting their adventures.

The footpath is covered with pink petals from the cherry blossom. It is slippery, like walking over pink icing. This big cake earth. I put fresh flowers all over a chocolate cake today – stuck in the cream and nobody here to eat it. Tomorrow Gordon and Woolfie are coming with Kate Morven and they like cake. All weekend I had no gas for cooking as I didn't know that without a gas pipeline, you have to ring up and have the cylinders outside the house refilled. Luckily I had an old electric kettle and an electric frypan so with a house full of visitors we had roast dinners and peas that were cooked on top of the woodfire in the dining-room.

The trees in the garden are getting greener by the day. Bugs and snails are eating vegetables. I have just come in from throwing tomato dust over things – a flurry of what looks like Johnson's baby powder ... dusting babies' bottoms.

When my son was here on the weekend we planted a white dogwood together. This way I get people interested in the progress of the garden and link them to it. Even if in the end a friend and you fell out, you would at least have a tree.

Tuesday, 22 October
Nineteen currawongs flew into the garden because I put some bread out. Darting around like trapeze artistes. Once fourteen

green bower birds came but nowadays only one or two appear. I am saving up the report for you of the blue male bower bird when he returns. He is a spot of bright ink from the sun. I can wait for him.

Today when I pulled back the curtains in my room I saw sunlight on lines of spiders' webs just as if they were Cupid's darts aimed straight at the victim's heart. I laughed and made a cup of tea ... glad it wasn't me.

Wednesday, 23 October
I have just been on the round of the garden. More beans eaten by snails. Gordon has gone to the shop to get snail killer plus food for our picnic. It is a white-and-grey sky with the sun coming out from time to time like a shy child.

The dogwood the Waterlily man and I planted a month or so ago is not straight. I pointed this out to him when he was here on Sunday, saying that it seems we can't even get that right. He said that it was done deliberately as it was in partial shade from the pine and would, in its efforts to reach the sun, turn outward away from the shade and so in the end, be straight. What can I make of that as a metaphor for our most hopeless affair? Nothing.

The house next door has been sold and so before the new owner came I dug out the small shrubs that were beginning to make a hedge between us and yesterday took them round in the wheelbarrow to my friend Sarah. We put them in to make a screen so she can sunbake. I want to be able to see into the neighbour's garden as it is wonderful with pale blue and lilac and pink alphine phlox as a ground cover under cream and pink azaleas and white rhododendrons. There are daffodils and bluebells and forget-me-nots in a wild random wave in a garden planted like a sea. The new owner only comes up for weekends.

Because I couldn't sleep, I got up at four o'clock and drank tea looking out of the kitchen window and the sky turned the very blue Van Gogh spoke of. Just before dawn, so blue with a single bird calling lost like a woman who has given up pride. Here is what Van Gogh says of this blue and the sky he once saw in Venice:

~ 13 ~

The deep blue sky was flecked with clouds of a blue deeper
than the fundamental blue of intense cobalt, and of a clearer
blue ...
In the blue depth the stars were sparkling, greenish yellow,
white, rose, brighter, flashing more like jewels ... opals you
might call them, emeralds, lapis, rubies, sapphires.

(*Arles 1888*)

I have this printed in a silk scarf of that particular blue
brought back from the Museum of Modern Art in New York by
some friends, Rose and Jack. I am wearing it now.

Thursday, 24 October
Snails fizzing like lemonade all over the garden. I felt so glad I
walked out with four packets of seeds and put them in the soil
with the snails lying about like overturned chariots. Oh my
revenge is sweet.

Kate Morven is washing up. We ate Russian Kruska for break-
fast. It is a blend of five cereals crushed the moment before
boiling into a porridge. It has a curious effect on me. I feel
invincible, as if I could bite a tiger. But I am glad someone else is
scraping the porridge pot.

On a picnic yesterday I picked a huge red waratah that is
here in a glass jug, tall, strong and bizarre-looking like a
Margaret Preston woodcut.

Woolfie, Kate and I have just walked round two gardens open
to the public for Spring. One was filled with rhododendrons. A
chihuahua came out of a door. The owner wearing a tweed skirt
and woollen hat, placed an old cream cushion in the sun for him.
I recognised the cushion as the one I bought last night at an art
gallery, in a dream. When I spoke of this to Kate she mentioned
a book called *An Experiment with Time*, by J.W. Dunne. I didn't
want that cushion when I went to collect it in the dream because
I saw it was only an old grubby thing and would look horrible in
my house. So in the end that dog got it.

Two green bower birds are flirting in the trees discussing, I
suppose, whether to fly down and try the contents of an old wok
I put out or whether the currawongs would chase them off.
Woolfie said as she brushed her teeth that it must be rather

like meeting the wild boys on your way home from school. The local bodgie gang. But just one magpie can put the whole lot of them to flight. Bullies are always cowards in the end. Although I often think the difference between a brave person and a less courageous one is that the brave have less imagination. In the bathroom I put a card Peri sent from Paris that reads: 'Considering how dangerous everything is, nothing is really frightening. *Gertrude Stein.*' That cheers me up when I think of my bills or a lover's desertion or his continual infidelity. Andy Warhol said that until he learnt to accept the fact he was poor, knew no one who was important, was an unloved homosexual and not good-looking (or words to this effect) he was miserable. But then he learnt to say 'So what' and his life changed. To be effective though, 'so what' has to be said often and with real conviction. Perhaps, like a mantra, it invokes the feeling.

When I stop, I hear two other typewriters working. Gordon is typing a play and Woolfie is typing her novel.

Here comes the rain again.

Kate has left to drive home to Sydney with her baby tucked into her seatbelt under her jacket. She knows it will be a boy as she had an ultra scan. When we went walking yesterday I saw she has stars in her hair. It is all scribbly curls and when the sun shines on bits of the red in it, stars glitter out as if they got caught. Seeing someone so happy is a bit like having a unicorn in the house. I lit the fire and now we have only one piece of wood left. More is due to be delivered any minute and it is now a race to coals. It is not serious, as there is the gas fire. I always think of the people who have been so cold they burnt their furniture. In *La Bohème* one man burnt his play.

Friday, 25 October
More rain. Will it stop before Christmas? Gordon and Woolfie left in a fog with rain drizzling on like a bad mood. I am cheerful enough; in spite of the strike a letter got through accepting a poem for *The Herald*. It's necessary to keep hanging on to things like this, these small events, so unimportant to the rest of the world, all bricks in a career it takes a lifetime to build. And here, like a flamboyant flag on the table, is the red, red

waratah. Big, bold, harlot of the bush.

Before they left for the city, Gordon, Woolfie and I drove to Katoomba, which I call Death Valley, as it is so cold. No typewriter ribbons of the right kind to be found, but when I went round the corner to the Denisons, David opened a desk drawer and handed me two. Fate sends me what I need in the hands of friends. Next, Fate, I need a kiss, heartily and lustily meant from that Waterlily man. Silence all week deep as the pond from him.

I walked home from the post office where I sent things to magazines, my red stockings wet and the rain pushing its cold fingers down my neck. Still no wood, but the wood man did call to say it will come.

I keep thinking of a red rhododendron Kate and Woofie and I saw yesterday. So red, lurid like a pornography of the garden. It also looked military, like the things you see at war memorials, even the leaf was like a laurel wreath and the red that of the ribbons. These bright colours are, I think, new breeds of rhododendrons. They are a mistake, orange and lurid red just don't look comfortable on that bush. Scotland's lanes are lined with wonderful purple rhododendrons, mile after mile as you glide your bicycle through them. They came first, I was told, from India.

Well, with this unceasing rain I decided there was nothing for it but to climb into a hot bath up to the shoulders in comfort, to keep turning the hot water tap on with a toe and to think BIG. The result of all that was I rang Christina Stead's literary executor, to ask him if I could meet with him to discuss doing her biography. He agreed without any hesitation to do this when he comes back from holidays. So, if nothing else was achieved today, that is not to be sneezed at. And this is how people enter prisons of their own making.

The tall, but half-grown gum tree outside the bathroom window gives me so much pleasure. On still, clear nights it sits with the moon about it like a Charles Long art nouveau painting. Today it was tearing itself apart in the wind like a teenager with a bad conscience. Tossing, not yet fully grown, so tormented and no one able to offer consolation.

Sunday, 27 October

The fire is just lit and my Father arrives here with this smell of newly lit smoke with a cup of tea for my Mother and we children stretching and fighting in our pyjamas. Outside the sea is rough, the dinghies pulling at their anchors like restless tethered cattle. I must find my school tie. My youngest brother Peter can't do up his shoelaces so I bend down and tie them. My brother Billy is wearing a grey jumper with black and white dogs on it that my Mother recently finished knitting. I am bringing out the hairbrush for my mother to plait my hair. I have two green tafetta ribbons in my hand that I am rolling to straighten. Next to the wheelbarrow and balloons, ribbons are the nicest things mankind ever invented.

The fire here is roaring and my feet are cold and wet inside my boots. Today I must work, as tomorrow I go to town to sign, at last, the Penguin book contract. So often in life, the thing you most longed for only arrives after you have ceased caring. Then that very thing you wanted comes up and taps you on the shoulder.

Work, work, what would we do without you? Plugging up the holes in my life with work as if it were wood and I a sinking ship.

It is very difficult to end an affair even if you know how utterly hopeless and destructive it is. Heroin or any hard drug, I suppose has the same effect. It is as if you have put a child into the garden, left it exposed to the weather, walked inside and closed the door. But no door keeps out the calling voice. This is no news to any one who has tried to give up a relationship without a quarrel. A psychiatrist I met in Wiesbaden told me he believes if you want something very much you set up a counter-force in some mysterious way that prevents you getting that thing you are so desperately needing. Perhaps there is something in that.

I see the blue lobelia and blue agathea that I planted a week ago have taken to their beds and are flourishing. Hardly any onions left though, and now the first big pink bud on a rose. Losses and gains.

On the way home from the shops I saw all the lilacs are out. There are three kinds here. White, lilac (the true colour) and a deep rose-purple hanging over fences like dark grapes. I have a jug of it on the hall desk. Stolen.

Yesterday when I told David at Snaps that I was thinking of writing Christina Stead's biography and that I had some misgivings about it (misgivings! I almost faint in the night at my audacity) he said, 'I think any person of a certain literacy and a gentle nature can manage a biography'. Strangely, I have quite the opposite opinion. I suspect it is one of the toughest, most arduous, taxing, vexing, terrifying pieces of work a writer can ever undertake. Let's hope he turns out to be right, but I feel certain he's not. Oh look! There's a break in the weather. Where's my coat? I'm off for a walk. Let the chocolate cake burn.

Later

Three friends have been to afternoon tea as they were here at a motel for a literature conference. I took them in the mist round the garden and showed them the two gigantic oaks in the bottom of my lane and the two white lilac just coming out. Also the last pink tulip ... the others have bloomed and gone. Just a few red petals on the ground like feathers a bird left after a flurry with a cat.

Monday, 28 October

Bus loads of tourists pass by like shades in shrouds of mist. Disappointed people going somewhere they can't see.

Two potatoes are through the surface. Yesterday a friend eagerly strode through the potato patch on her way down the lane while we laughed. Nothing was visible and for once I had no picture standing there showing what was beneath. It is a fact that if a plant won't bloom or grow you can sometimes get it to begin by harming it in some way. It is as if it lies there like an indolent woman stretching in bed, too lazy and secure to feel she must get up and act or life will pass by. So treading over potatoes does no harm, I suppose.

The two tall oaks in the lane are full green and buoyant. They are thirty-four years old, a neighbour told me. His children planted them.

Campanulas are spreading over into my garden from next door. Deep, bright and celestial blue; painters love it. Lydia stood one day beside that garden calling with her hands to the violets creeping towards my garden. It was the same gesture a mother uses as the child takes the first steps. She stands back, pulls her outstretched hands towards her and keeps repeating the gesture. People teaching children to swim do it too. Come over here, campanulas.

Madonna lilies I planted in the all white garden are now three inches through the soil. They are the flowers in Renaissance paintings that are given to the Virgin by the angel when she is told the news. They have a most wonderful scent. Here, beside the railway line, a version of them streaked with pink grows wild. Sometimes they are called Christmas lilies as they come out at Christmas time in Australia.

Well, I am off to Balmoral Beach to my old house that I shared with my friend Jean. She has gone to Bali for three weeks.

Wednesday, 30 October
Home with a tan. Tomorrow, Gordon, Woolfie, a friend of theirs and I drive to Adelaide to the Grand Prix. I am taking the lift to go to the tenth anniversary of Friendly Street Poets. Seven poets and I set up this poetry reading group at Andrew Taylor's house.

I have just bought Andrew's daughter Sarah something I absolutely love. It is a bride bear dressed all in white. It grasps things and hangs there like someone falling off a cliff. It may sound bizarre, but it is the most charming doll I've ever seen. It has a grip of steel, and soft ears under the white veil held on by a wreath of wax blossom. For years I had the piece of wax blossom my Father wore in his lapel for his marriage.

Tomatoes here sicker than ever. They look so like old rotting ships moored there by the fence slowly being eaten alive by rust. I am not in a good mood about the garden.

Mr Waterlily came to dinner twice at Balmoral. Although my strike (of a union with a membership of one) is nearly broken, I am standing firmish. There's no use pretending if you have an orange tree and you long for an apricot, that it is apricot. No matter how you cannot live without apricots and hate oranges, nothing will make that tree an apricot. It's a waste keeping on about it and besides you look foolish. Whispered phone calls while you sit at the table with a jaw frozen in embarrassment unable to swallow ... Sylvia Plath had to put up with that for some time until she left. You can't stop it, as far as I can see, except by blackmail, so leaving is the only way.

Thursday, 31 October
There is almost a full moon low now on the horizon. Dawn is coming through the pines like a tribe of Indians stalking game. Last night the moon came through the white curtains in my room like an archangel's torch. Strong and pure.

Today in the early light a reward and surprise. Three lilac and pink clematis out, big as stars hanging round the sundeck. I ran inside then brought Woolfie out in her bare feet and dressing-gown to see.

Now we are off to Adelaide and may heaven keep us safe.

~ 3 ~

November

Safely home after thousands of kilometers of wheat and sheep. Pale green wheat under the wind with ribbons of purple Salvation Jane along the roadside, tying up the paddocks like birthday presents.

My eighty-five year old Mother, in her living-room among the polished antiques said, 'Well, I'm ready to go at any time'. Packed, in a manner of speaking, for an unknown destination. Full of health, fulfilment and a curious acceptance of this step off a cliff she contemplates so calmly.

My brother, she said, had a sale of 20,000 sheep on that day. I have never seen as many sheep as that. She wept, she told me, at his first big sale, saying, 'All the time Daddy auctioneered, he never ever sold so many sheep from all the farmers round the district in one day'.

The first sheep my brother had were quandong stones in the desert where we lived. As the olive is to the Greek, the quandong was to us. It was our shade, our fruit, its stones our toys. We used wooden clothes-pegs lying end-to-end to make paddocks. The sheep were culled and counted in a narrow race made from pegs, the gate was a peg we turned from side to side. Later I sewed tiny bags from scraps of material and filled them up with wheat. I stitched the top the way the men sewed the bags at harvest.

Sometimes we were given toys. The boys got tools and I got dolls. My brother used his hammer one Christmas day before breakfast to crown my doll's head in a dent no neuro surgeon would have cared to mend. My Mother wept. 'It's Christmas, can't you ever stop your fighting?' I was not in a mood to be reasonable. I kept thinking that if I could just take the doll's head off, and push the dent up from the inside with my finger or a pencil, I could save her. But how to get the head back on?

We called at Leura on the way from Adelaide to water the

garden before going on to Sydney. My lawn is tall and could be reaped. I must get a mower somehow. The first roses have come. White petals around one bush like butterflies on the dry brown earth.

And now, the best surprise. The unnamed second stick of clematis I planted is blooming. A blue star the colour of the Virgin's mantle, streaked with a lilac wash. If a Madonna drew a star-shaped flower and coloured it with pencils, this is the colour she would choose. It's odd, these flowers that are so beautiful, and to me, exotic, blooming near some old wooden steps of no real charm. My plan is to drape the wood with the plant – in softening and disguising the steps, the plant will, in return, be supported by what it hides. Then I need a climbing yellow Peace rose to mingle with the clematis.

Pansies are out now in the new curved bed where the pine-tree once was. The soil is very poor there, drained by the tree, so as yet I think nothing much will grow. One pansy is a toy pirate ship's flag – white with a black centre shaped like a skull.

Down the lane weeds flourish. Tomatoes struggling on against a fate already written. Snails eat the blue pellets, fizz and die, and more arrive. Life! Inexorable, unmerciful, relentless, remorseless life. Beans sprout and burn out like sputniks. They seem to lack the heart for life. Fragile and delicate as premature babies. This nurse passes by feeling helpless, searching farther on for those ancient survivors, potatoes. The geriatric ward. Yes, there they are, a whole bed of them pushing up dark green leaves. Ruthless, inscrutable potatoes. My favourite vegetable. Overlooked, abused, despised, this humble tuber is the one I love.

Friday, 8 November
For a few days I have come back to Balmoral Beach, to the tree ferns, the shabby kitchen and the flocks of white cockatoos at dusk.

The blueing of Mosman has begun with the jacarandas stretching bluer than the sky's blue arch. On the way here, I collected *Vita* by my favourite biographer, Victoria Glendenning. Like her biography of Edith Sitwell, it's brilliant and I can't stop reading. At last, books that are not an effort to read. I've been reading *Vita* on the beach. There can be few more contrasting things than the life of an Edwardian English aristocrat and an Australian topless beach.

The water isn't cold. It's pale green, cool and clear and you can see your toenails when you stand to come out. This old wooden house has a pink ceiling on the cream verandah which is why I first rented it. It is surrounded by hydrangeas just starting to bloom. White, pink and lavender. 'We use them for funerals,' a Swede once told me, 'Australians seem to think highly of them'. Wisteria and honeysuckle make a jungle at the back hanging on the washing line in swags. Underneath white canna lilies among pink and orange patience. Everything is warm, lush and green. The washing sags in the damp air.

Tonight thunder shakes this house like an old wooden money-box. Over the sea lightning flashes its bad temper. I've always been afraid during these tropical storms that the stilts on which the house stands will slip and slowly it will slide down the hill in a deadly faint.

Saturday, 9 November
Honeysuckle scent is drifting through this window, fanned in by two tree ferns like giant green slaves. It's warm, the storm has gone, as if the play is over, the audience gone home, and today, the peaceful empty theatre.

The beach was crowded today because it's Saturday and now the back of my neck feels as though I have a hot scarf on it.

Sunday, 10 November
Bored, alone and idle, I wrote two poems. It's so often the way, when there's simply nothing else to do I'll work. Colette's first husband understood this well and used to lock her in her room until she'd written a satisfactory amount. Intensity and another way of being comes along and chooses you as its companion. As it sits down beside you, it lights a cigarette, points to the page and demands sternly, 'Write!' It never goes to parties.

Last night after dinner friends and I walked along the beach. The seagulls perched on the sharkproof fence as if it were a

~ 23 ~

necklace strung across the sea and they small pearls shining under stars. The Manly ferry floated past like a birthday cake with candles on its way to the party. We sat on the headland's bench and watched the sea and sky and held a little silence like a friend. They all left at twelve and I am here alone with the dishes. Not unhappy either.

Monday, 11 November
The Leura lawn keeps jagging at my mind like a ragged thumb nail. If I knew a man to pay, I'd hire him to cut that lawn. The clippings will be precious, I need a lot of mulch for summer.

More sun, sea breezes and the peace of living on one's own. Off to find a typewriter now, and later, to the post office. 'Put things in envelopes' is my motto. Did I get that from David Campbell, or did I simply dream it? It's stood me in good stead. At Balmoral the post office faces the open sea and the window holds umbrellas, hats and towels and buckets. On hot days, the Post Mistress, my friend Anne, has a swim at lunch time.

Wednesday, 13 November
I have been staying at Leichhardt. Today I came back on the bus to Balmoral. There, I admit, my strike of one ended, once again in defeat. But with red bougainvillea dripping from fences and verandahs and the jacarandas standing like blue hosannas, I felt doped on happiness. The Waterlily man lives in Leichhardt and I keep going back when I really should go forward.

Andrew Grafton came to lunch here today and we sat on the balcony eating mussels Portuguese watching an unknown bird, large brown-and-cream speckled like a hen, being bossed in the tall gum by two Indian myna birds. We are like two old people in a geriatric home, the others with whom we'd been so happy at the same table gone and not likely to return either, and we shaken almost to palsy by their absence. We swam after lunch and talked about our writing and our theories. After Andrew left, a wistful strange and unexpected mist came up from the sea like a sulky mood. And all the while, the sun shone down undismayed. Later I went out to post a letter and saw the mist had defeated the sun; the plants were wet with rain and above, like a promise, the first rainbow of this journal. I'd been feeling weak and useless as if I were a bathtub full of warm water and the plug had been pulled out. The sight of the rainbow, a bridge of air and pure colour over the bay consoled me like a kiss. And now bed, while outside a sky stained with pink like a blouse with a lipstick smudge and the sea pounding strong and regular as your mother's heart before you entered this world.

Thursday, 14 November
Have you noticed that certain meals are best in certain places? Anywhere else they are disappointing. Here, day after day I have a salad of nasturtium leaves and flowers with basil, parsley, lettuce, tomato and oil – nothing else, not even lemon. A few slices of cold lamb, green mango chutney, a hunk of bread and butter and pepper. That's it. Never was anything more delicious nor suited to this place. With a glass of moselle, I sit in my bathers and stare at the sea past the tree ferns and never wish for anything else.

It was the same when I lived alone on Crete and later Santorini. Every day I ate Greek bread, yogurt and tomatoes, cucumber, onion and olives staring out at the Aegean sea. Dreaming then of Homer, dolphins and a man in America I'd never see again. At night I'd have perhaps a piece of roasted kid or pork (lamb and fish were too dear) or some dried octopus, but everything else was the same as lunch. I was never healthier and ate nothing but this for weeks on end. I drank ouzo too.

Here at Balmoral after a swim and this meal from the plants in the garden, naked in white sheets still feeling the sun on the skin and hair wet on the neck, I fall asleep at once. That is what I propose to do right now.

Friday, 15 November
The cicadas in the ten thousand strong orchestra tuning up make me lisp when I speak. It's true, people who have no lisp acquire one walking along a bush track among deafening cicadas. (That is where I first noticed this phenomenon.) Lying here in the sun on the verandah, I couldn't now say 's' if my life depended on it.

A tall red kangaroo paw is blooming in a small green pot

beside me, its flowers so like feet you'd think an anatomy student, not a botanist, drew them.

My book *Luxury* arrived yesterday, with its two small girls in bathers on the cover, lying face-down gossiping on the beach. This sun is too hot; it's burning like a water-bottle without a cover so I must go inside.

19 November
Luxury was launched last night.

The night before I stayed with Peri who is, among other things, teaching me about gardening. In her pool at dusk I swam alone, I thought, until a big grey frog swam beside me. I tried desperately to rescue him until I realised it was his home. He was, in fact, the opposite of Stevie Smith's 'Not waving but drowning'.

Peri gave me secateurs and sent me into her garden to cut flowers for the party after the book launching. There were tall yellow and amber day lilies, ivy, white hydrangeas, foxgloves (*why* are they called that), white madonna lilies, and blue ageratum, love-in-a-mist, pink and purple fuschias: a real country bunch. Old-fashioned as a thatched cottage.

I bent down to smell the gigantic cream gardenia blooms and almost staggered back from the scent, strong as poison. A single bloom will scent a whole house. Here, with heat and rain and good soil and manure, the scent increases until they have the impact of a tolling bell. You sniff and reel and stagger to a white wicker chair and lie there on blue cushions until the scent diminishes and becomes what it is in common life, a gracious handclasp from a friend and not that buffetting and pushing from a stranger.

For hours Peri and I peeled a box of oranges. We boiled the zest, made syrup, sliced the oranges and reassembled them with toothpicks, and laid them in the syrup. It's an Italian dish and for three hours with aching necks, bent over the oranges, we gossipped. They were for the party. The best time at the party was the end when six old friends sat around yarning.

Wednesday, 20 November

I am in love with a weed. Its name is calliopsis. All along the train line miles and miles of the bright yellow flower with frail green foliage waving in the most brilliant display for a homecoming. Better I suppose to love a weed than a rogue. Home at last. Swags of white jasmine all over the fence and fallen on to the ground where the shed once was. Scent rolls in like waves.

The lawn fit for hay and, luckily, a man mowing in the neighbour's yard. I ran down and, yes, he was doing it for the money. He came up and cut the grass and now all the shape and perspective I tried to get is becoming visible. Pansies everywhere. Roses big as tea-cups. I picked some without scissors, too excited to run in to get some. So my fingers bled, as, wildly tugging at the stems, I heard the voices of my friends and my mother telling me to stop, to be careful, to wait. I have always been a bit fool-hardy and too impulsive otherwise those voices would not have stood there warning, pleading with me.

On this table is a cream bowl of white and pink ranunculi and jasmine and of apricot, pink and deeper pink roses. The roses are full as skirts, frilled with petals that, if they were at a ball, would swirl and sweep the floor.

Even the tomatoes have taken a turn for the better and developed some rustproof method and stand as if newly painted green just when I had turned my back and given up hope. Lettuces doubled in size sit among tall weeds thriving down the lane. Those weeds look rather like gladioli. You who are gardeners may know its name. It marches up my lane like ten thousand soldiers waving soft green swords. Potatoes sturdy and dour sit among the weeds. I have faith they will win their battle.

I have put out bread and seed for the birds hoping to win them back. I was always deliberately unreliable with them because I know it is a bad thing to make them dependent. I saw a black cockatoo on the way home today. I wish I could entice some into this garden. Wild, black and weird. Surreal messengers from Australian paintings.

21 *November*

Apples! Drinking tea I looked out of the kitchen window, just as I did the morning I decided to begin this journal, and there on the tree, I thought I saw nuts growing. I looked again and it is the blossom turned to tiny oval green and red apples. The air full of jasmine is staggering in the back door like a drunk after an all-night card game. I have been too excited to sleep. Pansies waiting for the picking. In a moment I am going out to do my round and to get a big dish of them.

How lovely it is to be home.

As I walked out at dawn to empty the teapot on to the camellias, the air was like vodka. So strong and pure a lungful can make you dizzy.

Visiting the Denisons this morning, to get mail they have been collecting for me, Lydia showed me old-fashioned roses in bloom. Grandmothers of the sturdy modern roses, they sit in their green bushes scented like the heaven they are planning to visit shortly. Lydia is going to give me some cuttings next winter so I can have some in my lane. It will be a guard of honour comprising Grandmothers. How happy I am in the Denisons' garden. Sometimes we sit in the wooden-summer house Mr Logan made for them and lean on the back of its benches and stare out either at the Himalayan pear-tree in full bloom or the daffodils waving under the birches or some other thing just coming into its perfection. We always walk around and they name the plants and describe what they will be when fully grown. New stone walls are being built so in the end the design will be a necklace of spaces linked by these beautiful ironstone low walls, all hand-built with patience and pleasure.

Today for the first time I began the worst job in a garden. Weeding. I took the wheelbarrow down as I felt that showed serious intent, and in fact, in a short time it was full of weeds. So I left it there to come in for lunch.

The tuberose bulbs are coming up. I dug one lot up by mistake and gently put them back muttering apologies as if I hurt a patient's bandaged arm. Oh, if you could smell this jasmine in the bowl in front of me, you would reel.

Friday, 22 November

Peaches. Yes, truly. Round on the side where the apple trees are, I saw a fruit soft and green like an almond. I walked out and there, sure enough, a peach tree fruiting. Pretty soon all I'll need are some chickens and a field of wheat and I'll be self-sufficient. Oh, and I'd like an olive tree too, while we're at it. And how I hope, hope, hope, the citrus in the back garden is a lemon tree. Suddenly it is sprouting burgundy coloured leaves and even, today, a flower-bud.

Yesterday, among the weeds and beans in the lane I decided to try one last count for my superstition of the number of beans and suddenly ... jackpot. Twenty-one on the twenty-first. Don't ask me why I was so pleased, I just was.

The Denisons came for coffee late in the afternoon and walked round looking at the plants. I asked the name of the weed so like a small gladioli and David told me. He said some nurseries round here actually sell the bulbs. It is the equivalent, he said, of a doctor selling capsules of bubonic plague. He makes me laugh. Lydia, a true gardener, weeds as she walks round.

The dish of pansies sits here on the wooden kitchen bench, their dark brown mouths so like children who have been eating chocolate at a party.

It is cold today, after two sunny days. I lit the fire with some of the new ton of wood Norm, the woodman, brought. Now for a walk to the escarpment to pay my respects to the Three Sisters, who keep their backs turned.

Saturday, 23 November

'When you're up to your neck in hot water, be like a kettle and sing.'

Doing just that in the bath I suddenly realised this song is not about taking a bath. For years I thought it meant that you should sing in the tub. The bath here is deep and old-fashioned and stands on curved legs on a slate floor. No matter how terrible I feel beforehand, that bath has never let me step out without feeling a lot better. Invincible, even, sometimes.

Snaps, where we go on Saturdays, is closed for three weeks so my friend Sarah is having us to coffee at her house. This weekend I am going to show her Buttenshaw Bridge which is nearby. It's across a deep gorge and leads on to Elysian Lookout, then to Olympian Rock then Tarpeian Rock. (Someone had a classical education.) I had to look up Tarpeian Rock in my Classical Dictionary. It is where the Romans threw people convicted of treason. All these places look out on thousands of acres of valleys full of gum trees. The trees, it is said, give off a blue eucalyptus fume and it is that which colours these mountains blue.

Today I am baking Cheese Roughs. I prised the recipe out of my Mother's memory when I went to see her at Gawler last visit. She handed me her old recipe book full of things that have won prizes in local shows all over the country. It is now coverless and half of it has gone. She'd lent it to a woman who let her child carry it home by the cover. If there was one thing my Mother had that I would have liked to be given, it was that book ... now it's almost useless. I kept on about these things she used to make until, later, she walked out of her bedroom in her nightie and said she could remember what it was. Cheese Roughs. And now they are in the oven rising like leaning Towers of Pisa.

If you want to make Cheese Roughs, put two eggs into a cup and fill it with milk and some cream, whichever you have most of. Tip that into a bowl and add two of the same size cups of self-raising flour. Mix that and add some grated cheese. Roll that out and cut it into slices about one inch wide and one inch thick and two inches long. Bake them in a hot oven until tan. Remove, split them and replace them until they are also tan in the part where they were split. Sprinkle with paprika and serve with butter. Hot or cold. That's Cheese Roughs, snatched from the grave as my Mother would say.

Sunday, 24 November
When I drew back the curtains this morning the sun was pouring yellow shafts through the pine trees into the garden. It was like drawing back the curtains and finding Eden. This is one reason why, I suppose, curtains are so useful in the theatre. There is nothing like a sudden revelation to take your breath away.

With a beginning like that, what else could the day do but go on to be splendid.

Sarah and I walked to Buttenshaw Bridge and then to Lyrebird Dell after going to Gordon Falls. It is not only Classical round here, it is nineteenth-century romanticism and First World War battles combined. Lone Pine Ridge takes you to Gordon Falls, for example. Wildflowers out everywhere, and among them we saw a tiny yellow honeyeater. I tested the water for swimming in the pool under one waterfall, but it is very cold. How I hope it will warm up soon.

Having coffee in the Denisons' gazebo, I watched blue-and-tan butterflies flit around like falling stars looking for the best landing space. They showed me their pond with the purple Japanese iris just coming out and around the edge, small wild strawberries, bright among their green leaves. Lydia gave me a foxglove in a pot for my garden, as well as powdered orris root for the pot-pourri I am making. Daily I'm drying rose petals and jasmine to put in the blue Burleigh china fruit bowl called *Calico*. (It is my favourite pattern.) I forget the whole recipe, but my daughter will remember it.

Well, I have been weeding and there is that same feeling of virtue now as after the ironing is done. I plan to weed a bit every day and, hopefully, get ahead of the growth and from then on manage it in a relaxed manner. We'll see.

The raddichio I planted from the Italian seeds is up and now is transplanted in a big tub, so I can run down the steps and pick some leaves just before I make a salad.

Is there any other tree on earth that suckers and seeds more than the bird cherry. I have dug up dozens of seedlings and still hundreds are left. The shade from one of these trees shadows the lettuce patch so I have been cutting it back with aching wrists. These wrists were meant for typing and now they feel like chicken bones.

Until this afternoon I did not know pansies had a scent. Putting some fresh ones into the dish I sniffed their smell like a baby's yawn. One blue one with a yellow centre is hanging over the edge of the dish just like a child hanging over the lowest railing on a jetty staring into the beckoning sea. Around the corner of the bowl its dark-haired sister is doing the same. What is it about babies that makes people feel they are so pure? My Mother said she always washed her face in the baby's bath water. She felt it might be good for her complexion. I sniffed my children's yawns as if angels' feathers fanned the air. I don't know why. Primitive instincts.

Monday, 25 November
Drat that it's cold. Last night I could wear silk to bed and now I have lit the fire. Cold Mondays are gloomy. There are plenty of jobs to do indoors, but who wants to be inside in November? I could unpack the books in the study, write to publishers, write up my diary (vacant for a week), pay bills with cheques that may bounce, iron, clean the cupboards, hope for a visitor. Some or all of that. When this fire is safe to be left, I'll have the best antidote to gloom, a hot, hot bath. Then we'll see.

A walk and a bath helped. Let me tell you about a tall messenger waiting for me when I came home from my holiday. Round the corner, near the herbs, tall and straight an iris in full bloom. Imagine the inside of a fresh mushroom turned into chiffon with a blue stripe, change this into a flower and add a tongue of tiger stripe up the side. Truly, I almost stood and cheered. What a welcome home.

Drenched. The sky has slit itself mid-afternoon and cars in the main street with lights on. Water rushing down the garden slope like a thousand running rats. Luckily, a lot of things in the post I was glad to have. A cheque for one thing, from the very publisher I was about to write sternly to on that matter. Proofs to correct. Then three calls from friends in Melbourne, as if they heard how cut off I am. Really, all in all, a marvellous day rescued from a ragbag of inertia.

Tuesday, 26 November
A rainbow last night bright as a halo. Sarah rang to tell me. I ran out and there it was, vast as God's bow.

Walking home in the rain yesterday, I stopped and sniffed. Claret jelly. There beside me was a portwine magnolia in bud. I picked some (naturally, my friends would mutter) and put it in a vase beside my bed. Old-fashioned claret jelly, in fact, smells more like it than port. Arabella Boxer, my favourite cookery writer on this earth, gives a good recipe for this dish.

Woolfie has arrived to stay a few days. It has been sunny for a few hours so the fire is out of place. Short of dousing it, there is nothing to do but try to look as if it is appropriate. It is not, as it is now far too warm. There is a stage in a baby's life that is like this. The child is too developed for an afternoon nap, yet from time to time, it's plain it needs one. That's what the weather is like now.

On the way back from Adelaide, we stopped on the banks of the Murrumbidgee for a picnic at dusk. Woolfie and I swam naked while cockatoos flew over. We told the men, from sudden modesty, to avert their eyes, and like two nineteenth century-gentlemen out with the ladies, they sat fully clad with their eyes turned down the length of the river away from us while we breast-stroked along in the cold khaki-green water. As we swam I told her the Chekov story of the Lady and the Double Bass Player. Leaving our clothes on the river bank had reminded me of it. We climbed out and slipping in the mud on the edge, dressed, got back into the car and drove another three hours to West Wyalong. Here we stayed at a hotel with wire coathangers in the plumbing. The noise grated irritably each time a guest anywhere nearby turned on a tap.

The pot-pourri is growing and now with more rose petals drying and some new petals bought from a shop in the main street, is sitting by the telephone in the hall and beginning to scent the house. One of the packets I bought today was labelled *Aphrodisiac*. Much good that will do here.

Wednesday, 27 November
What a marvellous day. And it's not over yet. Woolfie and I went for a long walk to Leura Cascades and back on a stiff climb to Olympian Lookout. We had coffee at Sarah's and came home, Woolfie to write, I to bake. I am making my Mother-in-law's recipe for caramel squares. Instead of dates and walnuts, I use pecans and dried apricots. I am making a hamper for a friend. Having the time of my life. Every now and then I hop on

the bike and ride off to the shops for something I need. Cardamom and rice flour and parsley. The parsley is for salsa verde, one of the nicest sauces in the world. Shortbread uses the rice flour and cardamom is for a sour cream cake. How I love a bake-up. The salsa verde is sitting in the blender, emerald green in its oil with six white hardboiled eggs on the top waiting to be blended in.

Saturday, 30 November
Breast X-rays. All clear. Each time this happens, I have an irresistible urge to shake the hand of the doctor who arrives in the waiting-room to tell me the news. I did this to this mild, civilised old doctor in Sydney. My daughter was with me and he talked to us both about breast cancer which is now almost an epidemic in Western countries. One in fourteen women will have it. The X-rays themselves look like photos sent back from a space ship. Distant blue-and-white photographs of earth attached to curving ribs. Oh Lord, I am relieved and so grateful. I have a shelf in the sunroom with a few books on it. Some days ago I looked at it and decided I would try to fill that shelf before I die with books I either have poems in or have written or edited myself. That is a good enough reason to keep living. Madly ambitious, perhaps, but it is better than despair and that, heaven knows, is never far around the corner.

I came home on a train with champagne from the Waterlily man. After all this time, I am learning to accept what I can't change. Marcus Aurelius put it this way: 'Take away when thou choosest thy opinion, and like a mariner who has doubled the promontory, thou wilt find calm, everything stable and a waveless bay.'

Today it was my turn to have friends to morning tea because Snaps is still closed. I like these garden morning teas better than the Snaps visits. But, in the end they would pall. A café keeps things more impersonal and also more public, imposing a discipline on the event that a garden doesn't. Because I am a single woman, I am nervous of living in a small community and fear being singled out for opprobrium or disapproval.

Three pink roses out and one white. Like garden-party hats on green stems too slim for their weight, they are drooping as if the wearers dozed off in the carriage home.

Everyone has gone home and I am alone with a bowl of pansies who keep their silence. Again the very thing I needed to read arrived in the hand of a friend. Yesterday on the way to the doctor, my daughter bought me Jean Rhys' letters. One of the great stylists of the twentieth century, I rank her with Nabokov and Colette. Self-effacing, edgy, hard to hold as water, she is the very texture of literature. All the while, unhappy, poor, excited, depressed, drinking, beautiful, hopeless, full of wit and a certain flavour hard to describe as vanilla. Rare.

~ 4 ~

December

Sunday, 1 December

The first day of summer. Mist creeps up the street like a burglar. Lydia and Philippa are going to an old-fashioned rose nursery about an hour's drive away. They invited me but I can't go because yesterday on the train home I invited a young American to lunch. He is backpacking around Australia and knows nothing of these mountains and had no map. I explained the way to the waterfalls. He has only bush telegraph to tell me if he is coming to lunch so I am saved from spending money I don't have on roses I long to plant.

I am baking Christmas cakes today as I plan to give edible gifts. David asked, when we stood at the shop counter together and I said I was buying the sugar for a Christmas bake-up, if I was sure I wasn't invented by Dickens. In fact, I think a Christmas bake-up only means you haven't got a great deal of money for presents. It helps too, if you like cooking. I hardly do anything I don't like. My daughter Caroline at high school was discussing with her friend Brigid what they might be when they finished their education. Caroline said she thought it would be ideal to do what her mother does. She told Brigid that I lie about all day reading books, writing poems and calling it work. Well, that's one way of putting it. Not too far off the mark either. I get very fed up with writers who complain they are not well paid. The truth is they chose to do this work and it's a privilege to have an obsession and there's no point grumbling.

Walking home with David I asked if a bush was a mock orange as it looked like one. He picked a flower and sniffed. When he gave it to me I said there was no scent so it couldn't be mock orange. He said that it was weaker from the mist and as the graffitists say, 'Mist Sucks'.

The American's name is Jim and he has gone back to the cave he found at Lyrebird Dell. Somebody's well-mannered son. He is off to India to look for what he does not yet know. Read Shirley MacLaine, sold everything and bought a cheap ticket to New Zealand.

It has rained all afternoon so I have had no walk. I was thinking as I lay by the fire that it is odd that with despair so close, for a person so attracted to heights in the grimmest sense, to live here has a real edge to it. I am surrounded by cliffs, precipices, gorges, leaps, lookouts, chasms and bridges spanning gaps. I stand well back while those who are not tempted or frightened walk right up and lean on rails. Woolfie often calls out to me as she leans right out over Olympian Lookout to come down and listen to the waterfall. No fear. My son has this feeling too. I deliberately never told him about vertigo so it came as a surprise one day when he was grown up to find he had it.

I am thinking rather anxiously of Jim out there in the cave in this cold, wet evening. He warmed himself so keenly by this fire. There is no dry wood down at that cave so he hasn't a fire. Maybe the path to enlightenment is meant to be hard, but cold too?

Monday, 2 December
I thought a bower bird. As I stood watching the birds come for the bread I threw out, I wished for a bower bird and there that instant under the birch was a female. Indian myna birds have come, drat it. They scare off all the others. I have found the name of the new big grey bird with red cheeks ... the Waterlily man showed me one in a book. It's a wattle bird. He rang this morning to say he will drive up with the boxes I left at his home as they were too heavy for me to bring on the train. It's mainly things I'd left at Balmoral in the rush of packing. Cake tins and suchlike. Now I need them because today I have two cakes to bake for Christmas. Yesterday's seemed to turn out so maybe I have got the hang of a new method. Now for twenty more. The very curtains will smell of Christmas cake before this is over.

How I wish it had been sunnier so that I'd weeded more. I want the garden to look its best this afternoon to show it off. It's half-weeded like a half-cut hairdo. Misty today so not a lot of incentive to kneel in the fog.

Last week I was paid by the *Adelaide Review* for a story. I have cash now for presents. Many people did not care for that story as it was written as a piece of female erotica. I think it was really a modern fable in the end. I warned my Mother that under no circumstances was she to read it. She had read my first book *Trader Kate and The Elephants* and was upset. Her fury was only matched, I think, by King Lear's. What a letter she sent me. I burnt it at once, though it was smoking as I opened it. In the end I replied saying I would write what I must as I was first and foremost obligated to it and secondly, lots of people who have high degrees (she would be impressed by that) use those words quite naturally and properly. No more was said on the subject. However, when I rang her last Sunday for her recipe for shortbread, I asked if she liked the new book *Luxury*. Coolly she said, yes, she had received it in the post and yes, it was very nice. In other words, she did not approve. Oh, well.

In this way women are censored by other women and the truth sits crushed under matron's skirts, popping out like a nervous mouse only from time to time. They all squeal then, raise their skirts and beg the men to kill it. Men might need censors, but women don't; they come with every woman writer as part of her family. Very few women write erotica. A woman has a line of chalk drawn around her just as if she was in a schoolyard, and stepping outside that, all hell breaks on her head. If she is unrepentent, she may be hounded out of the yard, ostracised and sent to Coventry. Then her only allies are men, and they in the main think they and their fellow writers are miles higher up the mountain than she is.

One man once told me that my poems were too thin in their shape. I mentioned this to a friend who is a painter. Immediately she realised the remedy and gave me a wide writing book. A different shape. I took it to Europe and wrote a book inside it but after three or four poems written across, simply turned the book up the other way and made it a long thin book. So, I am afraid, if that critic sees my poems, he will still find them the same gangly thin things like a schoolgirl. Knock-kneed and passioate.

Now it seems everyone's coming to visit. Angela Jones and Connie Fox on Wednesday. I am very excited so I have baked and cleaned all day. Here I am in a grey suit, all done up to prove somehow I haven't gone quite to the dogs. High heels are hell. All this and running out to put bread down for the birds so the Waterlily person can see the bower birds when he arrives. I will go back with him and do some Christmas shopping and return Wednesday in time for Angela and Connie. How I dread that drive down the mountain in all the traffic ... oops, I did not mean to mention such things in this journal. It is to be peaceful. If petrol even got a mention, I'd made up my mind it would only be in a sauce or flaming some duck or such ... not that it's possible ... please don't try it. I have champagne in the fridge ... here he is.

Wednesday, 4 December
Connie and Angela have just left. After lunch we walked in the mist but the whole escarpment was shrouded so they can have no idea that they were standing on the edge of a cliff over-looking all those acres of trees and space. I told them though. But seeing is believing. They say I seem calmer. I hope so.

Thursday, 5 December
A million kilowatts of sun drenching every tree and plant with light. Some one turned the lights on in the garden. What a day stretching away with only the most pleasant things to do. Feed the birds, write to publishers. The last not that pleasant, but helps my conscience and may, in the end, help feed me.

Connie rang up at eight o'clock to say thank you for yesterday. She really loves it here. Now if she saw it today she would never wish to leave.

Sarah gave a dinner last night. I have a headache. At midnight I found myself drinking port. I never have port. I don't even like it. I walked home up the hill with clouds drifting across the sky like puffs from a giant's cold breath over the pine trees in Leuralla. I noticed I was not walking quite as straight as I wished and seemed to be able to do nothing about it. Here we are, confessions of a lush. A new title. No, perhaps this will be

'The Illustrated Garden'. That is what one of last night's guests, Craig End, called my garden months ago when I first came here. I put little packets and labels on everything or nearby to show what they might grow into. It looked very gay and pretty, all the pictures of pink and white roses and pansies and poppies waving in the wind. When they blew away as they sometimes did, I ran after them and stuck them back on sticks or with a stone to anchor them. He walked down the garden and said, 'Hello, I see you have an illustrated garden'. Well, yes, in a way. When the flowers came, it was very wonderful to see the true thing blooming beside its picture just like a girl in her wedding frock standing by a photograph of herself dressed as a bride.

A big black currawong has come up to the railing at the top of the back steps, dark and weird, mysterious and yet cheerful. Sparrows are hopping about stuffing themselves with bread as if they were the Christmas turkey.

More Christmas cakes being made today. Blowflies buzzing round, the smell of the cake and that sound mean Christmas in Australia. Mr Waterlily said even my hair smelt of the cakes when he came up here to dinner three nights ago. This is one reason I suppose, that cooks wear hats.

I have been searching about for a new typewriter ribbon and asprin. Heavens, what a headache. I found instead, in a desk drawer, my daughter's skipping-rope. We bought it at Windsor when I took her to Europe for her fourteenth birthday. We spent the birthday itself in Paris in a Greek restaurant in the Rue de la Huchette run by Spanish men. Afterwards I took a photograph of her with the waiters and the cook. A tall waiter said to her: 'Now you must look as if you are in love with me.' That's Paris. Love elevated to religion.

Wrestling with a cake to get it out of the tin, it broke. Well, as my Mother would say, let that be a lesson to you. In other words, never ever use foil to line a tin. Brown paper is the thing.

Shortly I am going to listen to a tape my friend Gilly Sullivan sent from Wiesbaden where she is the resident lyric soprano. We were at University together and I have heard her sing in York in England, in Adelaide and Sydney. In 1979 we went to

Paris together and laughed so much in the hotel room we had to put pillows over our mouths. Frenchmen picked us up as she is very beautiful, and her blonde hair hangs down her back. She was too shy to speak French. Mine is almost non-existent so I made it up and kept shouting 'Non Disco' and so on to their mad invitations. Pressing, ardent, foolish, and a bit mad, these men turned up in cafés and on the street. Gold chains and hairy chests.

Friday, 6 December
Stay in your dressing-gown and you will get visitors. My friend George arrived at nine o'clock to return some secateurs. He put on Gilly's tape: Mozart and Verdi with the Wiesbaden orchestra. We listened and had some coffee. Next he gave me a lift to some bookshops so I could sell some copies of *Luxury*.

In the first one I lost my nerve completely and bought two cards instead. In the next the two women behind the counter looked dubiously at this little treasure – three years of work. A dead rat cast at their feet would have had much the same response. In the end they agreed to take three copies, on consignment, to see how it might go. I was so grateful I ordered the *Oxford Book of Australian Literature*.

George's car had stopped at Leura Cascades and we had walked the rest of the way. Even a bottle of pale pink petrol from a service station did not help.

At the place the car stopped, there was a small waterfall running into a stone basin on the side of the road. It was like Greece but here there was no icon or holy sign. George and I washed our hands in the clear water. I felt glad at this sudden bounty like a grace. In front of us was the valley and cliffs of rock leading away into the blue, blue distance.

We walked back to my house and had spaghetti marinara and claret. All the while Gilly was singing on the tape so it felt like a restaurant where people walk round and regale the customers. But better. As if a friend was singing as we ate our lunch.

Now to find out if my phone is working. I paid the overdue bill yesterday but will the cheque bounce? Publisher, publisher, send your cheque quickly.

Saturday, 7 December

Sun and birds whistling. I weeded a small, very small, part of the lettuce patch when I did my round this morning. Here is a rose. Pinker than watermelon on a long stem scented oh ... like a rose with dew on it.

How I long for bookshelves for the living-room, or this dining-room. Books are getting out of hand. Something must be done.

I had ordered a cabbage from the Village Store. Rode home with its great hulk, delighted as the boy who ran away with the pig under his arm. Jean with whom I shared the Balmoral house is coming up to stay overnight. Good.

I walk around my garden naming the roses. It sounds like someone calling their horses to feed – Carla, Pascali, Tiffany, Montezuma, Wini, Sonia, Gaytime ... Enough of this, I must go and weed.

I am making more Christmas cakes. The treacle I have poured would satisfy a giant. Now I am out of it so must go to the Store. What a place that is. A vast supermarket in this tiny town. Exotic supplies and yards and yards of deep freezers.

I have a theory that it is a secret supply base for an army hiding in the mountains. Outside, I once saw ten or so men loading trucks with boxes of food. All about was mist and silence. Where was it all going? How can such a vast place survive in this dot of a village? Who buys all the cans of chestnut puree ... the glass jars of pickled bananas ... the deep-frozen dim sims in packs so large it would need a barrow to lift them ... the kilos of imported cheeses ... the piles of gooseliver paté ... Only an army of gourmets I'd say.

But where are they hiding? And why?

Sunday, 8 December

Jean arrived yesterday afternoon. We walked down to Olympian Lookout and watched a kookaburra sit on the fence peering over as if contemplating the vastness of the blue distance and the millions of trees below in the most curiously human way. Below us was a sea of tree ferns looking from our height so like the small flat thistle weeds we had spent an hour digging from the lawn. Now I have my sore wrist in a bandage as the little instrument used for this, called a dab, needs the same action over and over.

Today we walked to the second Leura Fair. Last time it was washed out. Again today, two big downpours in between heat and sun. I got three old-fashioned roses and an aquilegea. We planted the roses as a backdrop for the modern roses as they will grow taller and bushier. One is called Jocelyn Flora. I bought it because I have a friend called Jocelyn. Another is a pale apricot rose called Lady Hillier (1910). The date, I presume, is when it was born, if that is the term.

We planted a *fica flora* (a red flowering gum) outside the study. A naturapath walked past with his dog and inquired if I knew where the river rocks in the front garden came from. I said I had no idea. He saw the gum and told me if I get a hive I can have honey from that gum. And, I suppose, from the jasmine in swags over the ground. Maybe I will.

This afternoon we walked to see Lydia and sat in her summer-house having coffee while a great beech bloomed in the sun like a blonde.

I am on the tenth Christmas cake and am going to stop. Enough is enough. I am tired of them. The cake tins look utterly battered. They have grown old this week. And me, I am a happy wreck.

I can't stop thinking about the naturapath. As he walked in the gate to look at the garden, he said, 'You have a sore neck'. I stared, thinking that perhaps he knew I was a writer. Writing and sore necks go together. After a bit, I asked how he knew and if it was perhaps the way I stood. He pressed one finger to the muscle and I still feel it like a brand. He turned to Jean and told her the same and added she has lower back pain. He put his hand on her spine and told her it was there that it hurt. She smiled and nodded. And now, like a prophecy, my neck aches and my shoulders feel as if the muscles have been used for crochet.

Three birds we saw yesterday are still flying past me. One, a bright red parrot, flew down to the bird-bath as Jean and I knelt weeding. We stopped and stared. A red to detach your retina. It flew away after a few minutes – swish – like a ribbon through the trees. Then, at the escarpment, two great black cockatoos, like giant bats flying across the sky. Huge, majestic and slightly mad. As if the Mafia pulled up outside your home.

Monday, 9 December
Here is summer in the mountains. It just walked in. Not exactly unannounced, but eagerly awaited and with many false rumours preceding it. On stage now, all in yellow light, a pale green dress blowing in a soft wind, birds in trees behind, singing right on cue. Above is a sky, blue without a single cloud, like a mind, so clear and lucid not one doubt encroaches. Hello summer.

Now what to do today. How delicious. No, I can't weed, the wrist is better, but three weeds would do for it. I smell of Dencorub and how glad I was to find it in the bathroom drawer left over from Caroline's rowing. It was beside Great Aunt Dorothy Venn's calamine lotion marked 'Miss Venn, 1958'. This family certainly goes in for history; it even keeps its medicines until they are almost archaeological objects. I could not give that bottle up. I am sure it is still perfectly good. One day I will possibly salve Caroline's daughter after a mosquito bite with it. If she has children, that is.

Robert Graves is dead. Long live his poems. A green bower bird flew down as I lay on the lawn reading a poem about a bird. So I wrote a poem about it. Out of the poem, back into the poem. It is, I admit, a frightening business not to be writing many poems. As if you earned your living skipping and even saw yourself reflected back from the world, as a skipper, and found one day you could hardly think how to do it. Then, when you try, you stumble. I think the great thing is to keep one's head and remain as calm as possible and know that it will come back. It's no good at all stirring it up making only turgid water. That's too disappointing and then you might really believe it had gone forever. Flown off like a bird.

The roses put in yesterday are not wilting so they seem to have weathered the shock. One is called Silver Star Café Rose. It says it is a lilac-blue. It isn't, it's a lavender-pink. I know as it has a bloom on it. The spinach is going to seed never having grown more than a three-inch leaf.

Tuesday, 10 December

Fertiliser. Yes, handsful of it. Yesterday I rode up to the shops and loaded up with a powder that is dissolved in a bucket and poured onto plants and another plain dry one. I strewed the dry one over the lawn as if I was a Biblical figure seeding a paddock. It is a beautiful action. Then I tipped buckets of the liquid fertiliser on lettuces, roses and anything else I felt needed it. I do feel it is cheating really because I read in a book that it depletes the soil in the end. What I really long for is a compost machine that chops up newspapers and other vegetable refuse. They do exist, I saw one advertised. The oak leaves are now covered by the weeds under the oaks in their full spring dress. So I must wait for them in the late autumn.

On a walk round Leichhardt a few weeks ago I saw a sign saying 'free manure'. I walked along as the arrow pointed and arrived at some stables. I was very excited and that night asked Mr Waterlily when, not if, he would bring up a few bags to Leura. He said he would never ever be doing that. But I do long for it. I never could understand how happy Peri was when a dozen bags of manure were delivered to her house. Just as glad as I would have been with a bottle of Diorissimo. I do understand now. Keep your Diorissimo, gentlemen, bring me horse manure and I will give you roses.

Yesterday I had to get the Denisons to come and stir in the flour for the last two cakes as my wrists are turned to jelly. They walked round at dusk and David stirred then tipped the mixture into two tins and now they are baking with the smell I know so well. And here endeth the cakes until next year.

I have been washing gramophone records this morning. Beethoven in the sink with Petula Clark. They are old records sent up from my house in Adelaide. Most too scratched to save, but some perhaps are all right. I see I had more modern tastes in those days. Most people, it's said, get more conservative as they grow older. I think it must be happening to me. You could say, though, that quality lasts and doesn't date, and weaker things show their faults.

Connie Fox has rung up and asked me to lunch at The Wharf in Sydney with Angela and herself. So I am off to town for a day or so. Gladly and sadly I am off to town. The satin bower bird has arrived. At dusk I stood at the glassed-in back room and there he was hopping about with his green mate. Dark blue like a satin cushion. Big and fat too, strong and bossy. Like an omen. I stopped crying almost at once. Things can't be too bad if you have a satin bower bird in your back garden.

Saturday, 14 December
Home again and none too soon. Three days in town from one friend's home to another – I am glad finally to be back. Connie and Angela gave me a present. It's Edna Walling's *A Gardener's Log*. Full of photographs of green draped space. It is, as I have said, her philosophy that is behind the way I am trying to build this garden. Formal shapes and strong structures hidden and draped with soft green things.

At lunch I ate octopus in herbs and talked nineteen to the dozen. I wear people out. I wear myself out. I am best taken in small doses. On my own I tire myself much less.

Woolfie and I sat in her courtyard one morning in our night-dresses drinking tea and talking about our lives and how our work was coming along.

I have picked a dish of pansies and six huge pastel roses, overblown as dowagers. White, pale pink, apricot and a deep pink. It took five hours to get home from when I left Leichhardt this morning. One train missed, one cancelled, a split in the track, whatever that is, and so on. Only the calliopsis waving beside the track and the fact I was coming home kept me going.

And, here, waiting, the Penguin cheque. I have it hung up like a dangling flag of hope over the kitchen bench. No, I won't be buying roses or trees with it; it is owed, dear, owed. And a lot more too.

An Emily Dickinson poems begins:

> 'This is my letter to the world
> That never wrote to me ...'

This journal is what I privately think of as my letter to the world. This book is for peace. It is a wand for calmness. I hope. At least, that is my aim.

Sunday, 15 December
Everyone has gone and I am alone with my sighs, the birds and the music. The sighs are for various reasons. Some best not analysed. A butterfly is folded into an apricot rose, and as if nature imitates art, the butterfly is caramel, brown and cream with dark dots among the edges of the frills of its wings.

A new man came and offered to cut the lawn. He has, and now I have more cuttings for the compost and the impression that someone has recently cared sits there on the lawn with its hands folded in satisfaction. Friends and I ate a salad from the herbs grown here, sitting at the table and chairs of the new white curly garden furniture under the bird cherry. I could see us, as if I hovered above like a camera. Set here in an Australian garden, straight out of Chekov. Birds, heat and speckled green light.

We walked down to Lyrebird Dell and watched the waterfall. The water is still too cold for swimming. A hand dipped in can tell.

Now, to be truthful, I long for a fog to come over to hide me for days and days while I lick my wounds like a dog. I have come back from the city, as usual with the feeling of a blade in the stomach. It takes several days to dissolve. One day, before this journal's year is out, that will not be so. I have faith in that. One day I will stop going where knives are not just kept in drawers. I'll go where flowers are handed out. I swear it.

Monday, 16 December
Dib dab. Dib dab. That dab is really a dib. I weeded yesterday afternoon. Weeding is so sensuous. It's hot and peaceful today. So far. Currawongs on the lawn pecking at the food. Bower bird, bower bird, come on back. Blue dot of hope.

Philip, who is thirteen, is coming on the train today. Heavens, how I hope he likes it here. It's the first time here without his father. Baking and fussing, I aim to please.

... Well, indeed I think I did. Woolfie arrived on the same train as Philip, so using the bike as a horse, we loaded it with bags and shopping and walked home together. Woolfie brought prawns so we had lunch under the tree. With lemon, fresh bread and butter and a salad with herbs, nothing more could have been wanted. Well, French champagne might have not been declined nor a red parrot or a lyrebird perhaps. Then we walked to the waterfall and had the first swim of the season.

A cliff of grey rock, with the water splashing down to a deep pool surrounded by tree ferns and bushes clinging among the rocks. Sand on the edge, with grey smooth pebbles farther in. It might have been designed by an environmental pool specialist. No longer does anything so wonderful seem entirely natural, but rather as if some person, not nature, made this perfection. I stayed in half an hour and so did Woolfie. We dried ourselves and walked home up the steep steps with thunder beginning to roll through the hot air and a few big drops falling on our faces.

Tuesday, 17 December
I bought the turkey today. Sarah, Philip, George, Woolfie and I had lunch of fresh pesto under the bird cherry. Why was I so happy? Why did Sarah say, 'Aren't we lucky... isn't this a heavenly place?'

George played squash with Philip in the morning and after lunch Woolfie went for a walk with him halfway to Bridal Falls.

I have planted two punnets of double petunias among those already flowering. If it works, multiply it, I say.

And, so be it, I hope, in this messy life of mine. Tomorrow, you see, with dread, off to the city I go. Paradise was a garden. That is what the word means.

Wednesday, 18 December
I have a hammock. Yes, a cream linen and lace hammock slung between the Japanese maple and the strawberry tree. A whole idea of indolence, luxury and romanticism in a piece of cloth. I bought it from a shop in the main street and rode home jubilant with it. And now, heaven send me poems to write as I lie swinging in it above the bird-bath in the shade.

Philip and I have had a long walk to the Pool of Siloam. He carried Gordon's bicycle down the cliff steps and up the other side. He rode on to see the golf course because he wants to learn to play. I tottered home after a few minutes standing, yellow skirt hitched up, in Lyrebird Dell pool. Ice on the thighs, heat on the head.

I have picked a bunch of pink roses to take to Mr Waterlily.

Speaking of the Pool of Siloam reminds me that not only are things named for classical times, or English Romanticism, they are also often Biblical. That pool got its name from the place where the blind man was sent after Christ daubed his eyes with spit and clay. He was told to wash in that pool and as he did, sight returned. And, if it had been this particular pool, what a vision would have greeted him. A tall waterfall, a deep pool of cold grey water, and behind that, trailing away, an overgrown creek full of ferns and trees filtering the green light as if sand was running through the fingers. In that creek are great boulders covered with dark green moss. If you climb down and go on you can take rests on these rocks, islands in the creek of rushing water, everything rooted in water, dipping in water, reflected in water. Overhead, through the branches, snips of sky and floating fragments of clouds. It is secret. It is sacred, perhaps.

Friday, 20 December
Now hell sends up heat. Hot winds breaking branches off the trees. I have been out in the garden giving first-aid. Petunias flat as dish rags. Even the herbs have hung their heads as if they've given up the ghost. Then the wind blew the front door closed. I had to break in through my bedroom standing teetering on a log putting my leg over the sill, never was there such a tall horse to sling a leg over. Grazed elbow and leg, plop down into the cool. Thank heaven for these old cool houses.

Mr Waterlily drove me up, the car buffetted across its track with the gusts. We found an air-conditioned Chinese restaurant at Faulconbridge and ate lunch and drank champagne. On to home and bed. Cool showers, iced water and very clean teeth are the things in this heat.

I am alone now, grateful for a visit to Leichhardt where this time there were absolutely no knife blades. Can it be that I am happy? Unworried, calm, tender with affection and confident? Yes, I think it's true. I have no more worries than an animal.

At times like this I feel as if I've been mined, given up jewels that have then been slung around my neck.

Saturday, 21 December

The cool change. In the night it crept up. Today, sun and a small cool breeze and the plants raising their heads as if the guns had stopped.

A good beginning to the day for me at least, because *The Australian*'s Literary Supplement has used a poem of mine. I'd hoped *The Herald* might use one too, before Christmas, but that is not be.

I have been down the lawn weeding. What a battlefield it has become. Blackberry and honeysuckle fighting it out with shell-shocked lettuces. I had hoped for a lettuce for Christmas. With only four days to go I don't think it is possible. However, I do have roses.

Tuesday, 24 December

Christmas Eve locked up in a lavatory. Yes, last night at dinner in Leura at a Chinese restaurant, I left Mr Waterlily at the table and failed to return. Locked in with a window to see valleys out of, screwdrivers passed under the door, a message sent to the table, and I stuck. The last one in the world adept at dismantling a door handle. The Chinese restaurateur, keen to save his door, instructed me in the use of tools in English I couldn't grasp, any more than I could turn the handle of the screwdriver. The calm voice of you know who arrived and told me what to do, I finally not only took off the door handle, but unscrewed two tight screws, dismantled the lock and freed myself. Now, if only I can learn from that and do it in real life.

Before dinner we drove to a nursery and bought a small Christmas tree in an antique brown pot. Here it sits now surrounded by presents and, with any luck, will be with me as long as I have Christmas. A tree is the most potent reminder of an event or a person, apart from scent, that I know. I wanted, I said, to turn this affair into a tree. Now I have the tree and the affair. And how tender, protective and gentle I feel. We wake, he leaves, I write, and now I must go to show Sarah how to stuff a turkey.

Now Hugh has arrived with his girlfriend Emily on a packed train, armed with red roses, madonna lilies and presents. His sister arrives in the morning.

I helped do the flowers in the local church this afternoon. It's my first civic act since I arrived in Leura. David had warned I might only be allowed in the back to work at the sluice. However, I was invited to arrange some flowers in front of the font. My artistic and symbolic arrangement of holly, red fushias with big white shasta daisies pleased me so much I had to restrain myself from rubbing my hands together. Holly for the thorns, holly for Christmas and holly to be a Christmas tree. The red fushias fell in an arch in the shape of a heart. The daisies were the stars. It was quickly removed and placed in a dark corner, where only by bending down with my head on the side could I catch enough light to see it. So much for religious symbolism and self-congratulation.

My next job was to copy an arrangement of hydrangeas, agapanthas and daisies. Mine was to be beside the organ. Sarah arrived, and mildly sneering at the copy I was to use, told me not to use any pink hydrangeas, only the blue and the white. (There are not many things on this earth more beautiful, I think, than a pure white hydrangea.) I took this mutinous advice, and leaving behind a masterpiece of blue and white with greenery pushing through softening the stems, daisies spilling down the sides in a froth of white, I rode home. Someone told me under no circumstances will that vase not have pink flowers before dawn tomorrow. We'll see. The whole event interested me so much and reminded me heartily of the six years I spent nursing. Hierarchies, hierarchies. Hell invented hierarchies.

Sarah and her daughter came to dinner with us. Taking the turkey from the freezer, putting the champagne in the fridge, hoping for satin pyjamas and no fights for tomorrow, off to bed.

Wednesday, 25 December
Happy Christmas. Emily got up at five to open her presents. I turned over groaning, thinking there is no peace even when adult children come home at Christmas. A sort of gloating groan. I made tea and we opened presents beside my most beautiful

small tree. Here's its name from the label – *Picea abius*. Hugh gave me two records: Pergolesi's *Stabat Mater* and some Vivaldi and Bach played on the cello. My favourite instrument. He got the season wrong with the *Stabat Mater*. That's for Easter. It is playing now. Margaret Marshall is singing:

> *While my body here is lying*
> *Let my soul be swiftly flying*
> *To Thy glorious Paradise.*

Hugh is out in the garden erecting the tent he has given Emily. He wants to take her trout fishing. She gave him a poster of Mick Jagger.

Red roses, dark as burgundy are on this table, the scent level with my nostrils. I sniff as I write. Now I must go to make the green mayonnaise to have for lunch with the prawns and then to stuff the turkey.

Thursday, 26 December

It's hot. Hugh has hung the hammock from the trees. D came to stay yesterday, and after we'd had lunch under the cherry, she fell asleep in the hammock. I have been out watering the garden and both the children are asleep. I want to go down to the waterfall and have a swim.

Last night we had Christmas dinner with turkey then a pudding flamed with whisky and with a whisky butter sauce, bonbons, hats – everything worked. At lunch time D swung in the hammock, straw hat tilted on her nose and sent out reason with the swing of the hammock. It is a good thing to have friends as well as family around on Christmas Day. Friends can be logical, families aren't good at it. Families smell kerosene and bring out matches.

Today Gordon and Woolfie have returned. Sarah came to lunch too. Hugh made tagliatelle with pesto and did an antipasto. All day the hammock was never empty and the day drifted past like a ship.

Friday, 27 December

I said 'Good morning, D, how are you?' She said, 'Have you seen the garden? How could you be anything but joyful. Last night we watched the moon come up'. (I had gone to bed early and only saw this giant white balloon rise through my curtains.

Woolfie walked into the kitchen to make tea and said, 'Last night we took our port for a walk. We took it to the escarpment and watched the moon'.

She dug around the apricot tree on the back lawn while we drank tea and I lay in the hammock. I hear that if you dig around a tree it will probably fruit. I told her that so she began at once. Apricots for next Christmas, perhaps. Hugh and Caroline and Emily went home on the train last evening.

Monday, 30 December
Mr Waterlily took me to Washaway Beach. We climbed down the rough cliff path in the heat with a bottle of champagne cold in a bag. There is no other access to this place and few people go there. Aboriginal drawings in the rocks lie wearing in the sun and wind, a tribal memory of the fish and whales and dolphins the people once caught here. The whole place has a magical and mystical feel about it and I never go there without being affected. It is secret, it is sacred, it's menacing and takes you in a gulp.

Today I came home with the garden parched even though Woolfie had watered it. Lettuces lie about not even fit for cattle fodder. I see there is more to gardening than planting, watering, weeding and keeping the snails down. How do people make a living from it? Even the wretched lawn is dying. One gladioli has a bud, that is my only positive report. But the petunias are blooming wildly and their smell at dusk as we sat under the cherry having a drink reminds me of the reason I planted them.

And now to bed. I do not recommend the city to anyone. Perhaps I should say, to avoid mystery, that the trip was harrowing and I saw such scenes only Edward Albee ever got accurately on stage. As a fig's stem juice curdles milk, so hysteria and shrieks addle the mind of anyone who watches.

Tuesday, 31 December
The apples have grown in the few days I've been away.

Woolfie and I stood drinking tea watching the sparrows fly around the tree. It is their tree. She told me about the moonlight picnic George gave last night on the golf course with candles adding to the light. I didn't go because even candlelight and the escarpment by moon wouldn't have cleared my head. Sleep did.

Three dahlias are out. Big, pink and spikey. It is so like finding out what frock a friend wears to your party only when they appear.

It is cooler and we plan a picnic or barbecue on the cliff if the council will allow fires tonight for New Year's Eve.

Ravel's *Bolero* is playing on the radio; it's what Hart Crane used to get into the mood to write. That and drink. He jumped off a ship and drowned and left the world poems. He is my son's favourite poet.

Yesterday I had one letter. It invited me to go on the Popeye cruise on the Torrens in Writers' Week in Adelaide next March for a poetry reading. Last Writers' Week they did a series of cruises and they were sold out. Chugging up the river, the boat laden with people and booze, drums began to sound on the bank. The pilot turned off the engine and we drifted in the dark with the river swelling and shining behind, all the world as if we were in Conrad's *Heart of Darkness*.

Afterwards we walked over to the Festival Club and I did a bit of high-class flirting.

Watering the garden calms me and pulls me back from the city. A painter friend said to me yesterday on the telephone that violence and hysteria are the opposite of creativity and that's why he can't afford fights. Well, words to that effect. I think there's something in it. I defy anyone to do creative work after a night of emotional violence.

Relationships can get a terrible inevitability about them that is obvious even to the people involved. As a stone runs downhill crashing and destroying, so does an affair gone beyond repair yet unable to stop until the final crash. It is sorted out then, once and for all, and the parties get up, lick their wounds and slink away to grieve and heal and to try again somewhere else. And that is what I hope will happen to this bitter trio I am part of.

Amen to that.

Now I lay down here for you a picture. An emerald green straw hat lying in an empty cream linen and lace hammock swinging slowly in a small breeze under a cherry tree beside a small birdbath where a green parrot is drinking. Does that calm you? I hope so.

Gordon and I have been exploring in his car to find places to swim. Woolfie stayed behind to work on her novel. We drove to Wentworth Falls and swam in clear deep water out from a sandy beach. There was a wind though, full of the dust of the desert of ages. So having swum with it behind us, to return it was necessary to backstroke or eat dust. In spite of this it is a real find and so close we can go often.

~ 5 ~

January

Wednesday, 1 January 1986

Happy New Year. Heaven help us all. Surrounded by a white fog when I woke up, just the red and green of the trees next door visible from my window. Yes, I did the appropriate thing; I burst into tears. Now the sun is out, Gordon and Woolfie are up and going now for a walk and I am making a quiche because Peri is coming up for the first time. I hate quiche, but we haven't got anything else to offer.

Last night Sarah, Gordon and Woolfie, Craig End and two friends from Sydney and I went out to the escarpment and lit a barbecue surrounded by tall gums and a white swirling mist. For some strange blessing, the mist stayed all around the area and through the tree tops until you could feel that the hound of the Baskervilles might howl any minute, but didn't come near our table. We walked home and Woolfie got us to dance in the street. I waltzed with her as she sighed and sang 'Oh, it's a white New Year'. The last I saw of her and Gordon were two forms, one so tall and one small, dancing at the crossroads by the letterbox as the mist swirled round them.

I went to bed and the phone began to ring as their drunken friends telephoned from Sydney. Then at two o'clock Connie and Angela rang from Adelaide. Connie gave me some sharp advice about getting rid of Mr Waterlily and trying a good woman. Wish I could. They are coming to stay in a couple of weeks so I must weed the garden and put on my glad rags. Blow quiche, I'm going to make pesto.

Peri has gone home leaving lots of day lilies to plant and a big clump of shasta daisies. The Denisons came to have a drink before lunch because they knew Peri years ago and David owed a gambling debt to Bob, Peri's husband. He'd bet Bob in 1972 that he and Lydia would never marry. Two years later they married. They'd even gone on Parkinson's TV show vowing they'd never marry. Peri left the ten dollars behind for me to buy a tree for the garden. Now that's creative gambling I'd say. David lost the bet, Bob won it, and I got the money, and the garden got the tree. I plan to buy a tulip tree because when we walked to see the Denison's garden, they described what a fairly small tulip tree they have will be like soon.

Thursday, 2 January
A hot day after a moon last night like the gold half-closed eye of a fatal Greek god. Staring through my window at my face on the pillow, strong enough to give a burn. A lunatic night. Sleepless.

Today is hot and I've been weeding the white garden. For lunch Woolfie steamed vegetables and amongst them, the first leaves of the garden's spinach. It's too hot yet to put in the plants Peri brought up or the white gardenia and the red azalea I have in a bucket of water that Sarah gave me from her garden, where they were dying in thin soil. Last year at Balmoral there was 'The day the gardenia died'. It shrivelled in terrible heat. Later it resuscitated in water and is now flourishing in my white garden. Now here is another to try to save, so perhaps recovery and growth are really possible even in the face of what appears inevitable destruction.

As I dug up these two plants from Sarah's garden I talked to them saying they were being rushed to hospital and all would yet be well. It reminded me so much of the day I first took my son to kindergarten where he lay on the floor and sobbed. I told him he would like it there and he said 'No I won't. I'll hate it.' Finally he did learn to like it and it took about two days. Everyone and thing seems to loathe change even if it is for growth. Myself included.

Lying in the hammock, swinging it by pulling on the cherry's branch, I suddenly realised it was very like a relationship. It can only work well if you let go and then return because holding on with a firm grip or clutching leads to no movement at all. It is the hold and release that makes the hammock swing.

Friday, 3 January
White fog swirls round the house like a mind full of sleeping

pills. White and beautiful like death.

Last night Gordon and Woolfie left and Mr Waterlily arrived. With the fog around us we sat on the front verandah this morning while he drank a cup of tea and I rested my head on his shoulder. He was waiting for his car to start which it finally did.

I sent some poems off yesterday to *Scripsi* and the ABC as a show-of-work flag for the New Year. *Helix* and *Southerly* have accepted the same poem and I am not sure what to do. The fact is, having had it for six months, I feel responsibility might be placed on their shoulders. Australian poetry would improve greatly I think if a magazine editor or two were actually paid.

Today is the day to plant the day lilies, the gardenia and azalea and shasta daisies. The fog can be their anaesthetic. I must borrow the Denison's spade as I have none.

They comfort me, can't say how. Oooow I'm wondrous sad.

I thought I'd drowned the waterlily. Yesterday I noticed the level of the pond was low, and not thinking, filled it with the hose. I saw the lily underneath the water, drowning with its leaves upturned like faces trying to reach air. Today, though, it has floated up and will, I hope, survive. I wrenched some ferns away to give more light as I'm told it won't flower here unless it gets a lot of light and sun.

Saturday, 4 January

Ah to wake in the arms of one's love. Is there any better way to start the day? If there is, I do not know it. Here is peace and may heaven help me keep it.

Another dinner at the Chinese restaurant last night. Mr Waterlily and I walked home with the stars above. Soft cool winds like heaven's silk shirts swirling around us. At eight this morning he drove home.

I have been to Snaps today. David and I walked home with the bicycle, my steel horse on wheels, coming with us.

Yesterday copies of the layout of the Penguin book arrived. The galleys come in two weeks, they say, on my birthday. I sent off poems to magazines because I was full of despair. I was determined to make something of the day and in a month or nine some will come back with perhaps a note in accepting one or two and the day will not entirely have been wasted. 'Redemption through work, Love Kate.' That, a friend said yesterday on the phone, is on the postcard I sent to her from Queensland, months ago.

Now my friend Ron Pratt is arriving on the train from Adelaide. He has been Headmaster of an area school hundreds of miles out in the desert for three years. It is at Tarcoola, near the Western Australian and South Australian border. He will stay a couple of days.

I must ride to meet the train.

Sunday, 5 January
I told Ron to go outside to smell the air because it will almost snap his head off like a shot of vodka. He loves this place. It is his first trip to the mountains. He asked me to buy a paper on my early morning bike ride saying, 'Do you realise you hold a unique place in my life?' I asked why. He said, 'Because you are the only person who has ever managed to make me forget to find out what won at the races'. He said yesterday that if he could positively have a guarantee that heaven is like this he would consider returning to the faith. He makes me laugh. We were on a walk round from Olympian Rock to Elysian Rock. There against a blue sky with frothing white clouds, with the mountains below, stood the sign like a direction to heaven *Elysian Rock*. I showed Ron how to set off little pink trigger plants with a fine piece of stick as Mr Waterlily had showed me yesterday. As the bee's proboscus enters the centre of the flower, whoosh, a green curved trigger flies out spraying pollen like a yellow puff of smoke from a stormy sexual scene. The bush as a Western.

My first spade. I got it from the Village Store. The owner didn't know the price but said he'd tell me later. If it's more than fifty dollars it will be returned, shop soiled, as they say. Jean came to lunch with a friend and David, Ron and I had lunch then all set to work. The day lilies are planted. The gardenia, azalea, shasta daisies, foxgloves, and hellebores went in also. The justicia friends gave me was planted among the petunias and if half of this lot take root I'll be grateful.

Surprised too.

The first lettuce went into the salad. Not much bigger than a child's fist, but as Ron said 'There is probably a market for bonsai lettuce somewhere'. Bitter and small, but all this garden's own work.

The man came to mow the lawn today. Ardent, interested and keen on gardening theory, we talked a bit while the coffee boiled dry. He thrust his hand into the compost heap deep and low, brought out a handful, smelt it as a man sniffs a Scotch and held it under my nose as if I were a favourite horse. It smelt like earth so it must be working.

Monday, 6 January

Ron's gone. He left behind stories of Tarcoola in fifty-three degree centigrade heat and his school that serviced an area of 40,000 square kilometres. Fettlers swinging drunken fists at him and his staff, dodging blows and finally teaching them to read and write. Horse races where every jockey's drunk. A brutal landscape with a majesty that he said has marked him forever. When the temperature went down to forty after a hot day it felt like a cool change. I am going to my birthday party with Jack at Kirribilli. Each year for the past fifteen, we have shared our party. With a mind slow as mud from writing poetry I hope to act quick as water.

Tuesday, 7 January

Oh happy day. What a party. What a night. What a wild thing. What a dance. What a lot of drinks. What a duck. What a restaurant. What an old friend. (Jack and I had our party, as you may have gathered.) I swam at six-thirty this morning in the pool where he and Rosie his wife are staying at Kirribilli. Mr Waterlily drove me home tonight and now he is watering the garden and all is well with my small world.

After dinner a dusk walk to the escarpment. Blue dusk pouring in over the mountains like memory flooding back. Rosellas darting like flames through the blue. On the top of a tall pine on the way there a red king parrot swaying and calling like a bear on a ball in the wind.

Wednesday, 8 January
Currawongs calling as if rehearsing for a concert by the Academy of Ancient Music. Old songs. Six in the back garden, black as a medieval torturer's thought; they fly up, sway on a branch, sweep down, fly and sing and call. Welcome bright day streaming through the trees. And behind, in the tall distance, dawn sliding down the pines like a pink silk nightdress.

The blue car drove out and down the mountain very early. Alone with the birds and my work. Glad too.

These contrasts suit me. The peace of the garden then the frenzy fumes and fun parlours of the city, then the quiet where only branches and birds make noise.

I am reading some of Flaubert's letters. Flaubert the sensual intellectual. Few ever cared more about style than Flaubert. And think with what ardour he struggled and made the pure perfect style of Madame Bovary his own against every natural inclination of his pen.

Thursday, 9 January
Fat apples. Will the possums get them? The sparrows are flying in and out from the tree bringing no harm. If birds were given human tasks, sparrows would suit getting children off to school with packed lunches. They are so busy, so cheerful, and so early.

Martin Philips and Andrew Grafton are coming today. Both are poets so I'm dragging out all my recent stuff to show them. They show me, I show them. Yesterday I sent off ten envelopes of poems and also learnt how to put the chain back on the bicycle. Also planted hollyhock seeds. I got them from a plant as I passed Kirribilli.

Friday, 10 January
Andrew and I walked to the Pool of Siloam this morning. I am flat like a tyre. I am rolling along like a hoop. Soon I will begin to wobble. He is as easy to be with as a good dog. We had veal liver and sage under the cherry for lunch and talked about trying to write a novel. Who can maintain that energy? He says it needs a mind that can think in great swatches. The overview.

Talk about character ... think of Flaubert toiling away at

Madame Bovary for five years! Truly I know the short burst of poetry suits me better. It's the difference between a marathon runner and a sprinter. How long have I been asked when I will write a novel. Poetry is in many people's minds kindergarten, and university is the novel. Sometimes, in my weaker moments, I think they're right. I haven't got a novel in me. A man called Rafferty has just run across the Simpson desert. I took a walk to a waterfall.

I have a new diary. Andrew brought it up from town. It's a Letts. The best kind. It's my twenty-first diary. Why do I do it? Because nothing's real unless it's written down. Also, if someone says something is not so, I do not need to feel crazy, I simply walk to the bookshelf, take out the year and open it. Documentation saves me from feeling I might be sent to the madhouse. It's my anchor, my truth, my secret, my confidant, my supporter and the order in my life. Saved by words, that's me.

Martin went home last night after a walk to Olympian Rock and watching a bushfire at Echo Point. Helicopters were dropping water on the fire. Smoke instead of fog swept over the Three Sisters. Today it is clear as a slate wiped clean.

Tomorrow Elizabeth, who is eleven, is coming to stay for a day or two. She has crept into my heart like water into sand. I can seldom think of her without tears coming to my eyes. I am not sure why. She dresses up in my old ballgowns. Dancing and swishing round the house in mushroom pink taffeta with a mile of skirt, a boned top, sleeves dropping from shoulders, knowing that indescribable feeling a woman has when she knows she looks beautiful. It is power, it is luscious, it is happiness, it is swish and swank. Oh, bring back the ball and the dance and great dresses I say. Earrings swinging, a neck that grows two inches, a back that straightens, feet that long to flirt, a skirt that swirls, and men who are willing to die. Terrible, deplorable and wonderful.

Saturday, 11 January
'It's been pretty dry lately' as my Father and his friends used to say. The lawn is dry as a blotter. I could sign my name with the hose.

Andrew went home after coming to Snaps. I feel so unused to being alone I'm like a dog wandering about disconsonately when the owner's away. And yet how much I need this time. I can't write much when people are around. I can only talk about it.

Sunday, 12 January
Domestics today. Luckily I like it. A clean-up purifies me like a swim. Piles of books out that now I must find places for. I unpacked boxes because David said one woman was whipping another in a photograph of the Mardi Gras New Year's Eve at Katoomba in the local paper. It reminded me that a friend once said there is probably nothing in modern life that, given two weeks, one couldn't find in classical Greece or Rome. There is a mural of a woman whipping a woman in a Dionysic rite in the Villa of Mysteries at Pompeii. It is one of my favourite things in antiquity. I got out books to find it to show David. There it was, the wonderful old red walls, one woman being held tenderly by another and a third winged woman with a whip scourging her for some reason all accepted and understood in the mural, but a mystery to us. The mural makes most sense if it is read as a continuous narrative as if it is a film clip or a set of pictures done in the manner of a comic strip. It is full of action and movement and music. One boy is playing a drum, another a set of pipes, and one woman is dancing with castinets.

I have just been down the lane. You won't hear me on lettuces, tomatoes, potatoes, or even onions any more. You will see me at the shop.

Blue and white are the colours coming out now. Agapanthas (*agapae* means love in Greek) that I tried to hard to kill are blue hands of bells on long thin green wrists. Blue hydrangeas all down the drive too. And with these, the white gladioli. I picked the first one two days ago. Odd to think I came here to starve out love and tried to dig up the agapanthas as a weed because they are so prolific and could take over everything. Nothing worked. The agapanthas bloomed, love stayed. 'Nothing else in nature behaves so consistently and rigidly as a human being in pursuit of hell,' Pete Townsend says in *The Horse's Neck*. He was talking about heroin addiction, but as

Helen Garner points out in *Monkey Grip*, there's precious little difference between that and an obsessive addiction to love.

Elizabeth, her brother and father arrive tonight. Never a dull moment.

Monday, 13 January
Three big king parrots eating small red apples. At seven this morning as Elizabeth's father and I stood drinking tea, he pointed and there, as if just finishing dessert, and about to call for the port, were emerald green and red parrots making an end to my hopes of apples. I ran and took photos through the window.

Elizabeth slept last night in the hammock, the lace over her face to keep off mosquitoes. She came in though, at two, because a cat wearing a bell prowled round. Beforehand we sat with her under the stars, her father and I, while I told her the story of Ferdinand the bull. My favourite story ... the bull as pacifist. Stars like the eyes of planets peering through the blue curtain of the sky. It feels so close here you could stretch up your hand and pull the curtain across.

Friday, 17 January
Home after my second birthday party. A sudden electric storm just as my friends were arriving. On the back lawn at Peri and Bob's, white petunias hailed down from the top-storey window-boxes. A rain of flowers. Peri said 'What are you going to make of *this*?' I said, 'A lot'. Now I really do think it was an omen. The black threatening sky with lightning shocking across it like a fit of bad nerves in the dusk and then suddenly a rain of white flowers.

We went inside and had turkey and a baked ham in a dining-room like a maharaja's tent with Indian glass candle-holders two feet tall on the table. What did I feel ... edgy, yes, that's the word ... edgy ... who isn't at their own party. Grateful, and even that warm smile that comes from actually feeling liked. Sheridan, Peri and Bob's daughter, made a birthday cake and when my friends sang I actually felt happy and pleased. Caroline stood beside me giving me a hug from time to time and as I plunged the knife into the cake after blowing out the candles, I held Elizabeth's hand and made a secret sad wish.

Last night Mr Waterlily arrived and we played the new record of Carl Orff's *Carmina Burana*. If there is anything in music more marvellous to make love to I do not know it. The notes on the cover say 'Primitive, evocative, and even obsessive rhythms combined with simple formal melody...' The texts are taken from a thirteenth century manuscript ... and they recapture the lost world of the rebels, or simple drop-outs, song, celebrations of a very earthy Venus. In a record such as this, it is not only the singers, but the sound that is crucial. Not the lovers, but the relationship.

Now, rain for two days. The garden is drenched and I am grateful. It is greener and roses have fallen with petals in a fall like cut silk to the earth and even the parsely is taller in a mere three days. The whole of the garden or life change so fast only a camera or a novel or diary can make the changes visible. Otherwise, it all seems slow and ordinary. Not in fact much change at all. Hour by hour the changes happen. Chart it like a candle's flame.And how do you give up a relationship when all night both of you are the river and the river's bed and neither know the difference.

Saturday, 18 January
Fog and rain. Fog and rain. All night it rained and today I stood looking out into the back garden; the poplar is standing in front of the pines surrounded by a swirl of mist. Death is a lady. The poplar stands there like a beckoning woman to the line of soldiers whispering 'Come on. Come on into the line of bullets.

As I went out to bring in the paper, a currawong flew over low carrying a piece of ham I'd put out. The bird was like a plane skimming low, trying for height like Biggles.

Today my old friends from Adelaide, Marisa and Philip, are coming to stay. I am making turkey soup.

I've been thinking. What if the whole history of romantic art and literature is merely the chart of an addictive drug? And with this pearl, I'm off to Snaps.

Sunday, 19 January
Sunny, sunny day. All the colours of the oracle of autumn are coming. Nothing here is ever merely green. Burgundy and lemon, cream and yellow are always splashed through shades of green with all the flecks of nature's eye.

Philip and Marisa walked with me to the waterfall and left last night. Today Caroline has come to visit with her friend Jim.

I slept in the hammock while Will made lunch. D gave me a book on Jung for my birthday and it was that I was reading as I dropped off sinking into sleep under the sway of the hammock.

Caro has a haircut that is so short her head is the same shape as it was as a baby in her bath. It grips my stomach, it looks so vulnerable. Lovely to rub your hand over hair so short, sensual and sweet, like a puppy. She was hard to give up. If they don't leave, you haven't succeeded, but I did not wish her to leave. When she was five and in the school Nativity play I asked her what she was to be. She said she couldn't remember. One night sitting in her bath she called out that she remembered what she was: 'An angel!' I said, 'Type cast' with all the fervour of a mother's bias. Now the photo of three angels in white sheets with cardboard wings sits on the bookshelf. One was blonde, one a redhead and the other a brunette. Caro works for the Nuclear Disarmament Party. Peace and its politics are her concerns; mine is that police are forever hurling her over railings. Don't they know they are throwing an angel around?

Monday, 20 January
Kookaburras have been laughing in the top of the pine. It is impossible not to ask at what? Paranoia makes you think they are laughing at your own folly. Fancy being miserable in this heavenly set-up.

I've picked roses with dew on to make a new pot-pourri. Now I have powdered orris root to preserve the petals. Mr Waterlily is coming to stay tonight.

I have just ridden back from the street where I bought some running shoes. They make you feel you could fly. I don't run but stroll. I look American.

Some days are hard to get started. This one is stalling and where can you find a day mechanic. I must must must write the Penguin poets' biographies for the anthology. But I can't. Would a drink help? I don't think so.

Gordon and Woolfie rang up to say they are going to live in Greece. Sarah is moving back to town. So that leaves the Denisons, the winter and me. Postie – bring something exciting. Redden this grey.

Thursday, 21 January
Silence. How hard it is to bear and how little we get of it. Here I can have it sometimes if I want it. I play music instead. Is it the fear of the abyss? Why did my Mother, having reared four of us to be the most silent children, suddenly when widowed and living alone, start to bang doors and pots and sling cutlery down the table in a din that amazed me. (The reason she wanted us to be quiet was because noise made her feel ill.)

Never have I seen so many birds as in the last few days. I look up and there they are flinging themselves through the sky like hasty arrows. I never see the bowsmen. Last night, five or six huge black cockatoos were in the pines as Mr Waterlily and I walked down to Olympian Rock. They were eating the nuts from the pine cones and dropping cones. I don't stand under pines nowadays. Weird, weird birds, calling like tortured horses. Red king parrots also in the pine trees and red-and-blue rosellas bathing in the guttering on the back of the house as we sat having a drink in the garden. About twenty currawongs on the lawn and hopping from branch to branch feeding on the leg of ham I put out. Wattle birds and myna birds and sparrows. I lie in the bath and watch them. Medieval people were fascinated by birds because to them they represented freedom. Is that why I am suddenly so keen to watch them while I feel so anchored and paralysed.

As I sped home on the bike yesterday wearing my new fancy running shoes, I passed the geriatric hospital and saw the people sitting on the verandah with their rugs around their knees. How soon, I thought, I will be there anchored too and now how happy to speed by wind in the hair, knees pushing up and down with the lovely free thrill of it. Bikes were made in heaven.

I used some of the lettuces, shooting up to seed like yachts slumped at low tide down the lane. Chopped and fried in butter, put in a pan of chicken stock and green peas, with some cooked rice, it's Arabella Boxer's Spring Soup. Well, a variation of it. Cucumbers are nice fried in the butter with it too.

Blue, blue, blue. Down the drive, blue hydrangeas and blue agapanthas make an aisle fit for a bride. I take the bin down the path with the flowers standing at the side of our procession like a Greek chorus draped in blue. I have been round to Sarah's to put her bin in and there I picked some even bluer hydrangeas and put them in a glass jug here on this glass dining-table. They are the blue of heaven's skirts. Their blue is from iron and the defeat that real beauty brings to eyes that see it. Something in you must slink away in the face of it. It's a blue that slays. A blue to slit your throat.

Wednesday, 22 January
Bridal Veil Falls at dusk with Mr Waterlily yesterday looking for lyrebirds because they come out at dusk and dawn. Black-faced shrikes in the gums, but no lyrebirds for us.

Connie and Angela have arrived by bus after their train broke down, struck by lightning. With them is their English friend. Now such an electrical storm, the burglar alarms are set off all over town. Rain coming down by the tankful. If the whole of the state is flooded, here I'll be among the last hundred to go. It'll be time to call Noah if it floods here. But it feels as if it could at the moment. I am using a candle as the light has blown. I have always thought the weather was the world's most boring topic and here I am writing a book on it. In fact, I hated talk of the weather so much that once when I was having an affair with an Englishman in Adelaide, he spoke of the weather at lunch and I stood up and said I was leaving because if he was reduced to that, we plainly had nothing left in common. He looked startled and said that the English think it a fine topic.

Thursday, 23 January

Last night Angela, Connie and their friend and I went to Balmoral House to dinner. It is an Edwardian house painted pink with bentwood chairs in the dining-room and lace curtains that veiled the white fog through which trains passed like diners' dreams. I felt I might have been on the Orient Express with trains passing going in the other direction. There, they have a chef who actually likes herbs and used them in every dish. I know because I ate everybody's herbs. Sometimes I feel I could go out and graze, I long for greenery so much.

We came home through the fog in a taxi with the cliffs swirling below like my head. Then we listened to Gilly's tape of her singing Gilda in *Rigoletto* and Angela read a bit of this journal. Now I must write fast because my readers have caught up with me. It feels like being one step ahead of the sheriff.

The first fire of the year. Damp wood, dry paper. Now I must put some wood kindling under the house to dry for winter. Connie's steamed pudding is on and I have rung my wonderful bank manager to see if I could have another thousand dollars. As usual he said 'I can cover you', whatever that means. But he said it might end up being twenty per cent. It seems to me money is getting very expensive nowadays. I rang because the living room curtains are finally ready and need to be paid for.

I have just taken Angela to the waterfalls. We have come home with red faces and now will soon be hotter because, oh my, is this curry a hot one. I plan to leave my children equal shares in the big bag of chilli I got in Dixon Street last year. I put a tablespoon or two in the same curry and had Mr Waterlily groaning half the night. He says he has gastritis. When I get upset I toss a lot of chilli into the curry and dye my hair hellfire red.

Friday, 24 January

The big clean-up. Now we are sitting clean and happy like good children by the fire. In the morning we all sat on the bed and laughed till my chest is sore. Connie and Angela have gossip to an art form. Outrageous, malicious misfortune to be gossiped about by them. Connie says 'Mad people who laugh a lot' describes themselves. It is so like my four years in the nurses' home. Their friend is sitting here doing a set of regional Scottish accents that are hilarious. We went to Smyth's restaurant in Katoomba last night. I ate cappacio (raw meat) while Connie shaded her eyes. Mist and fog are swirling round and now how I long for a walk if it lifts.

Tomorrow these women go and I will miss them like a tooth. My tongue will go to the hole and the day will be empty. As I feed the currawongs the remains of the turkey, Connie stood watching as they flew down saying 'Oh, aren't they ugly birds. Will they hurt you?' These, my black trapeze artistes, callers of my days.

Saturday, 25 January
The hollyhocks are up and my friends have gone. We went to Snaps this morning and came home down the Mall and they got their things and took a taxi to the train. I have been swinging in the hammock and wondering what to do. Umm ... ummmm ... ummm.

Last night we played charades. Connie got tired so finally we did it in her room while she lay in bed laughing. Angela and I were a team and she acted 'The Year of the Dragon' to the others while I believed she was acting 'Lucia di Lammermoor'. No wonder she looked so unnerved and puzzled.

The sun is out and the garden soft from rain. Yesterday if a dove had appeared carrying an olive branch I would not have been too surprised. It had poured and poured day and night hour after hour as if it might never remember how to stop.

'And now' as Mrs Dickens remarked when funds were lower than usual, 'I must exert myself'. Something must be done about my finances, and quickly too. But what? Mrs Dickens decided to open a school. But in spite of a large brass notice on their door, she never had a pupil and finally the man came and took away the notice because it was never paid for. I think I am good at cleaning. Some may not agree, but I do.

I have been thinking, as you may be able to tell, about Dickens and so on. I have never ever understood how people discovered, apart from being told so at school, that books were actually about something other than words. It was not until I went to

~ 70 ~

university that I discovered that you were not expected to just read books, but to think what they were trying to say. The secret message. All my life until then (and I was thirty-five when I got to that place that was so happy for me) I had read and read every moment I could snatch and was reared to feel guilty about reading. In my opinion that is quite a useful thing, as it adds a zest to the whole matter quite unavailable from virtue. I kept wondering how people ever discovered that, say, Dickens or Patrick White were trying to say things. I may sound odd, and as if I was a bit dim, but I don't think I was. I thought it was the same as going to the sea to swim. You opened a book and read. Simply floated through the book hypnotised by the words. When it was over, you closed it and didn't read it again for a while. It could, though, be re-read at any time as it was simply reading. I expect I got my taste for the stylists from this method of reading. So Jane Austen, Rebecca West, Chekov and so on were the books I read again and again. If there is no message, there is only in the end style I suppose.

The Zefferelli film of *La Traviata* has just finished on TV. It's my favourite opera. Outside a full moon is swinging like heaven's lamp through flitting clouds. Underneath it, beside a river, Mr Waterlily lies in a tent not alone.

Sunday, 26 January
Light mist with birds calling. Early in the mornings the orchestra tunes up and each bird with its different instrument begins until, grouped or alone, they mix the sound into a great texture that nets up the lightening sky.

All these things console me.

If you want to know how I bear these weekends where the sacred bourgeoise Saturday night is spent with someone else, I can tell you. Three things. Practice; the knowledge that she too joins me in knowing what it is to have the devil spit on us; and that better women than I have endured it with dignity and silence.

These are the *reasons*, I tell myself, but the truth is I have agreed to it. The stark wooden fact that stands like the pillar of an ancient jetty, refusing to rot, is that I have agreed to my powerlessness. It is of little comfort to know you have only yourself to blame for your condition.

And now I am off for a bike ride. If you are sad, go into a garden. I don't think anyone ever came in from a garden sadder than they went into it. But often calmed, distanced and consoled.

I have been around to the Denisons and had coffee in their summer-house with two of their children, who are visiting during the university holidays. Lydia showed me two framed embroidered samplers she has collected. One made this year, the other in 1822. Beautiful like tiny gardens.

How hot it is and I made a fire this morning so with all the windows and doors open, I sit with sweat running down my legs. As I've said before, there's only one thing worse than having a fire on a hot day and that is not having one on a cold day.

On a walk to Buttenshaw Bridge I heard a small frog in a pool where there are miniature native violets. I crept up on him twice, but each time he heard me and stopped. My eyes are not as sharp as some people's. I see that when I go walking with Mr Waterlily, for example. He sees and stops and points as I lumber past. We did not invent the world, it was invented for us by our relatives and friends and teachers. Oh God, it's hot in here.

I was so tempted to bring you back a native violet to lay here on the page for you to see. (Don't worry, I never pick wildflowers. A friend here does and they look beautiful in her living-room. We don't share the same ideas on some things. When she saw I was shocked that she got them from the bush, she said that if God provided, he would provide more. We don't say that about our bank manager though.)

Monday, 27 January
Seven-thirty on a foggy day. Apples getting fatter and it's Australia Day. All over Sydney people are dressing up as convicts and colonists, celebrating what must surely be one of the world's most ignominious beginnings for a nation. No re-enacting the shooting and poisoning of Aborigines. No ritual mixing of flour and strychnine either. Guns and flags and hats. Enough, enough ... my mood must be grim. I see my liquid paper correction

fluid has a notice that inhaling it may be dangerous. Oh glorious mankind. I must go for a walk and find a way to begin this day in a better way.

I am superstitious today. I always believe that superstition can be measured as a factor to the degree of powerlessness the person feels she has. It is no coincidence women have been guardians and connoiseurs of superstition in our society. Amen.

Connie has just rung from Adelaide to say that they liked being here. Good. I liked having them. When will I laugh that much again. Pretty soon I hope. George has left to go to the Sydney Dance Company after lunch under the cherry of spaghetti marinara. Thank heaven for a deep freezer and marinara in big cheap packets. George is a mathematician who is interested in ideas from the, well, less logical side of society. Einstein, he said, and Niels Bohr, two great physicists, came out at the end of their infinitely complex theses saying contradictory things. One said that there is nothing else, and there can be no faith (in anything I assume); the other said there is now only faith.

George just spent fifty dollars and a day at the University of New South Wales on a course on astrology, was bored witless and left at afternoon tea-time feeling quite depressed. I don't wonder, but then I haven't got his open mind.

I have been out picking the heads off the basil. Is there any sweeter smell than basil on this earth. My hands smell of it. Taking off the seeds keeps it growing. Basil, king of herbs. Basilica – king's house. The Greeks keep it outside every taverna and carry it out from church with bread on feast days but, as far as I could see, don't eat it. I offered it in salad to a Greek boy I met who whitewashed houses on Crete and slept on the beach. He said, 'I do not trust it'. He came to dinner in the house I rented for a month and he had the manners of a king. He and his friend Carlos taught me Greek dancing in the dusty street outside the taverna. Carlos kept saying, 'Look me' as I protested that I couldn't do it. Later people in the taverna broke plates while he danced like a satyr among them with bare feet.

Goats and chickens lived in the dusty main street and there were no shops. I sat at a tiny table with them when they asked me as I passed by and they wouldn't let me buy a drink. That is why I asked them to dinner next night to try to repay the hospitality. Carlos had only about four words in English. 'Look me' were two. Pannos knew a little more and I had only four words of Greek. I once wished the goatherd who passed my house each morning 'Happy Christmas' but he corrected me and explained I meant 'Good Morning'. I was so isolated but on the whole the people were good to me. One day a woman came out of her house that I passed each day. She made a cup with her hand to show me what she wanted me to do and into my hands she poured almonds. I said *'Evcharisto'* and together we smiled, she went back into her house and I climbed the hill to mine.

When my Greek landlord George heard I was having two local men to dinner he nodded and did not say anything. I asked if he would take me on his trip to Heraklion to visit his mother so that I could buy Greek cakes. We went, with George playing country and western music very loudly on a tape and crossing himself as he sped past churches at a great pace in his Alfa Romeo, with old women and their donkeys swerving off the road to avoid this monster so like Toad of Toad Hall. I said, 'George, you may think all this crossing yourself will keep you safe, but the way you drive, the law of averages will combine to make you crash'. He said he had never had an accident and did not think he ever would. I have worked in intensive care but said nothing more. George was a gold merchant with a shop in a vile town called Aghios Niklas, near the village where I stayed. He had white leather shoes, gold chains and nice manners.

At the end of the day, I made a Greek dinner, the two boys from the beach came and were drinking retsina with me because they said the ouzo I had was far too strong. I had got it from a hole-in-the-wall shop and when I first had it before dinner days before, my legs had turned to licorice and I had had to go to bed without dinner. They said the ouzo was not what they had in the tavernas. Suddenly George arrived. He'd driven twenty miles from his home just, I believe, to see that everything was all right. Nothing was said, but I remember it.

I wrote a book while I was in Europe on my own for four months. It's called *I Am My Own Companion* but strangely, my nerve failed me and I never had the courage to send it to a publisher. I felt perhaps no one would be interested in what I saw in a female Odyssey round Europe.

In all that time alone in Europe I only had one really bad experience. That was in Paris with an American from the Village, he said. He showed me horrible photos of his girlfriend, then leant back like an evil Pope and accused me of being puritanical. It took four showers and lunch next day in a beautiful restaurant on the Boulevard St Germain with a half-bottle of champagne writing poems to recover. It reminded me so much of Henry James, but in reverse. The New World was what I had found corrupt; the Europeans had been fine to me.

I met a young French poet when I went to a concert. The man next to me realised I had no French and explained a little about the concert to me in English. We had coffee afterwards and he said he was a student and a poet. He asked if I had seen the Monet show that was on at a private gallery and offered to take me. He said, 'I will show you my Paris'. And he did. The Monet exhibition – it was the waterlily series – was on in the Marais and each room had been decorated to match the paintings. In one room, with paintings, it was all white with Debussy's *Spring* playing and the true scent of a garden wafted in from vents. Then lilac, pink, green, lavender and blue rooms and small bridges in some of them. Australian curators would find it excessive I think, I liked it. Then we went and had lunch with a ceiling of mirrors and green palms around us. The way Frenchmen do not shave for a day or so is very stylish and looks not at all debased, but is, in fact, a compliment.

When Philippe heard I was leaving Paris, he said he would come to the airport. I said it wasn't necessary but he said it was not good to leave a country without a friend to say goodbye, so he came in the taxi with me to the Charles De Gaulle airport. There we drank some German beer and said goodbye and I have not seen him since. I did not go to bed with him, nor was I invited. Sometimes we write. He gave me his book but I couldn't read it because it was in French.

And what if, when this King of Infidelity Mr Waterlily rings up, I say, 'Oh my noble Prince, sirrah, get thee hither' wouldn't that be fine. But I won't just yet. I haven't yet the courage but do read on because one day it will be your and my turn to cheer.

Have you ever noticed very few men have the nerve to act as they do without being guilty. They often behave like the Marquis de Sade crossed with St Paul. It creates a lot of confusion but its main design and effect is to stop Mummy getting cross.

Tuesday, 28 January
More rain, drat. All my knickers got wet on the back balcony. These details. All my life I wanted glamour and now I am much more interested in rubbish bins and the washing. I am making a cult for myself of worshipping the ordinary. Mince, bikes, pansies, old fences, these are what I like now.

Yesterday George took my bike to get the chain back on because neither he nor I could. Today I must walk to the post office in the rain to send off some poems. I only wish it was a film script ... and how the thousands would roll in. Oh, a wet day, no money and Mr Waterlily has just rung up having been away with his mistress ... aaagggghhhh ... I must have another cup of tea and pull myself together.

Gilly wrote from Wiesbaden. I had just walked in from posting a letter to her, a big part of a manuscript. How her letters cheer me up. Nothing in my life is as difficult as hers. Isolated, lonely, working always with strangers, struggling on from audition to audition all over Europe and singing role after role with the critics and their pens at the end of it all.

I am making pesto to freeze for winter and the smell is everywhere. It's a simple recipe. Just two or three cups of fresh basil leaves ground in a blender or pestle, with three or four cloves of garlic, a cup or so of oil, half a cup of pine-nuts and a cup of grated parmesan cheese. That's it. Pesto freezes well. Never try to heat it on a stove as the cheese cooks. Instead, defrost it then add a ladle of boiling water from the pasta on which it is to be served.

I thought about jumping off Buttenshaw Bridge down into the cool green miles of gum trees, but decided against it. Things will definitely get better, and soon. I feel it. I'd be so mad if I was lying there and a big offer came from a publisher.

Wednesday, 29 January

It's raining. The radio is playing Ravel's *Pavane for a Dead Princess*. Today I must bestir myself. I just looked down at the floor and there, from the archaeology of paper, a studio photograph of my Mother and myself has floated up. My Mother is in a dark green woollen frock with silver beads on the collar and a few scattered over the shoulders. I remember it. I am about nine months old in a white dress, with smocking on the chest. She is holding me, or perhaps sitting behind me while I sit on a table at the height of her chest. She has a look on her face I never saw. It is of sweet, trusting adoration to the person behind the camera. I look alert with one hand out, I am trying to figure out what is going on. I am enjoying the party atmosphere and the attention. My mother would have been pregnant with my brother Tom by the time this was taken. She had four children in five years. All the rest were boys. The photographer has put his signature at the bottom: 'Keith Murray – Pt Lincoln.'

Now I'm off to the post office again. Sun's out, things might be all right after all.

Later

And now the moon like the half-closed eye of an ancient witch glowing through the branches as if it has a pterygium tells me I will never see the world unless I cut out what must be cut out.

Today, in the garden in a fit of energy I cut back cotoneaster and finally, the ivy growing through the art nouveau air-vent in my bedroom. I have watched it grow from two green heart-shaped leaves going in such a hopeless direction. More and more leaves followed, paler, thinner and more hopeless. I lay on my bed and watched hour after hour, day after day. Now they aren't there. One snip and a tug and they were gone. I brushed against the prunus and cut my shoulder as I did it.

Thursday, 30 January

Hot and windy today. No one has been here since Saturday. I got some wood from the escarpment yesterday at dusk. It's time to start getting in a load while it's dry. I wrap it in a towel now, it's my new method and I think I remembered it from old paintings of women gathering wood. You use the towel like a ribbon around the sticks.

The birds are bringing out their young. The babies' heads are still fluffy and they are as noisy and bossy as their parents. Yesterday I thought I saw a pair of bower birds in the back pine tree. I only hope it's true. I couldn't get a good look but these were bigger and rounder than rosellas and not as big as the currowongs. When I came here in June they were not uncommon.

Now I am off to look up my medical book to see what ails me. No, it's not my heart, that's plodding on whatever I wish.

And now the final ignominy; a sty on my eye. That, and a midday movie and drink. I never got this low before. Let's face it, men aren't faithful to women like me. I'm not pure as the driven snow myself. But, even if I remind myself of the triviality of my situation compared to say starvation, car accidents, real tragedies, it does me no good. The fact is I have knitted myself into a real corner and now I must turn the corner or unravel the whole mess. A sunny day and not at all sober.

Friday, 31 January
Hooray. Caroline has been admitted to the University of New South Wales. Last year at the beach with Mr Waterlily he opened the paper and her name was not on the list of acceptances. We sat at lunch time on some rocks and ate prawns and drank wine and I kept crying. That night Peri took me to dinner at the Hilton to cheer me up. She said when I had recovered, 'I never saw anyone so easily cheered up as you'. Well, after two brandy crusters, a lot of beautiful wine, and a rare steak, who wouldn't feel a bit better. I had cried enough. After a while, you can't cry any more for a time, at least. This past week I have done enough so I have stopped. Now a sty in each eye.

Today I've hung paintings and partly cleared out the study. When you have large swatches of time alone there are no end of things you can find to do rather than do what you ought to do. Next I think I'll try cat's cradle in my hammock. All this to avoid doing a task I truly dread. At least the house looks better and not quite so stopped, as if the owner heard some news as she was unpacking and left hurriedly.

When I first came here I painted almost non-stop for two

months to make it lighter because with all the dark wood and the stained doors, it felt so gloomy. I knew if I didn't do it at once I'd soon get used to it and never change a thing. Four coats on intricate shelves and edgings kept me quiet for a while. I wrote almost nothing – could barely write up my diary.

I often think about the man I heard of in America who, having a deadline to finish something for a publisher, complained to his wife that he had no peace in which to do the work. She said she'd take the children to Coney Island for the day so he could finish the manuscript. When they tottered in at seven in the evening they saw him just putting the finishing polish to the silver he'd been cleaning.

Well, it's happened. The galleys have just come for *The Penguin Book of Australian Women Poets*. On a rainy day in the country, having a nap, the doorbell rang. A courier with a parcel. My heart is beating faster. I held in my hand the result of an idea I cooked up on a Sydney ferry two and a half years ago. All because when I came back from Europe I got very fed up to read that two poets had published an Australian anthology and, having only six women out of twenty-nine poets, explained that they had looked for the women but had not been able to find them. I vowed then and there I would make a book so that no man could ever say that about Australian women poets again. And here are its insides.

A great white cockatoo flew past soon after I opened it in the sun room. It flew close to the wall of glass and away off into the pines in the fog. Naturally I took it as an omen. It was so big it was like an albatross. This book has been like an albatross itself, plagued with delays and difficulties. I am all the more moved by that to have it now so close to publication. I might add that the thing that really got me raging about the statement by those two poets was that while I am quite used to hearing that women are not good enough for publication compared to men, it was a new and bitter twist to say we didn't exist. They did me a good turn as without that I wouldn't have dreamt up the book. From your insults I can make books. Now I must ring my collaborator and get ready to proof-read. Hell and damnation.

~ 6 ~

February

Thank God I got through January. D has come to stay the weekend. Three o'clock in the morning and D and I listening to opera. Great excerpts. Cut out the boring bits, listen to the highlights. That's what I like. Then I told her lots of home truths and came within a hairs breadth of betraying half my friends. Many of them are related to each other one way or another and as Richard Tipping would say, it's like a shoebox full of grasshoppers. You need to be very sober and very careful when you discuss people and the past.

Sarah and I saw two films in Katoomba at the Community Centre yesterday afternoon, sitting on upright chairs muttering like two old women. Then we went to Smyth's and D came too. I had some French champagne given to me for my birthday so we had that and a right royal talk.

One of the films was called *Dance with a Stranger*. I am still thinking about it. The other was *Burke and Wills* which I am not thinking about. Give me the sound of the heart's murmurs, not the sound of horses' feet.

It is warm and windy. I have hung the hammock for D to lie in when she gets back from her walk. Half a gallon of marinara sauce is made because Hugh is coming up with Emily, bringing the curtains for the living-room that have cost an emperor's ransom. The problem was I ordered them from England last June and then the dollar fell and their price rose and rose.

D has just come round the door in her emerald green long shorts and bright blue shirt and my brown Frenchman's sunhat singing, 'Take a look at me now, in charge of who I am and where I'm going' ... doffing the hat as she sings and doing a small dance. There is a note of irony; she's reading Jung and hoping to discover something. Goodbye, sweet D. She's divorced and rearing three teenage children alone.

Pretty soon in this journal I am hoping to use more colons. Some writers use them often. Along with semicolons, it gives a sophisticated look to a page. Watch me try soon. I think of sentences as maps rather like a line drawn that traces, say, a walk or a creek. Some writers make the most wonderful lines. Alice Monro, for instance. As she puts all these lines one by one together she makes a life drawing and it is called a short story. It is the story as a map.

I was never any good at literary criticism. I never had the strength for it. I have partly earnt my living by it; another of life's ironies. But it always seemed a brutal business to me. I had to take valium at university each time I did an essay on some writer I liked. It had an operating theatre aura about it, the work lying there on the table and the critic delving in among the intestines looking for God knows what. No, I never cared for it. Either a thing is good or it is no good and that's the end of it. I was though very, very jealous of all my friends who could do it so effortlessly and so well; they were dancing and I was a cripple hobbling down the corridors of the English department crying, ashamed and envious. It's a skill I admire greatly and writing in any society is usually only as good as the critics are capable. Lousy critics, lousy writers.

It's too hot to go outside ... for the first time since I've been here I have had a fan on. Jean came too with Hugh and Emily and she has helped me hang the curtains in a temporary way. Things are getting pretty posh around here; curtains in every room. When it snows they may keep the heat in as they are lined with a type of rubber on linen.

Hugh came down the lane with me and picked Emily a bunch of the bubonic plague plant, watsonia. It is a burnt orange flower and looks beautiful. My hair feels hot and I keep splashing water on to my face.

Monday, 3 February
Wet and foggy. Damp air that isn't cold and this is the day to begin the biographies for the Penguin book or never speak to myself again. Everyone has gone home and a cup of tea, the typewriter and the birds stay with me.

Last night I got the new day lilies in with Hugh's help. He

dug a hole by the side path with the new spade and the new fork. I found the lilies on a walk last week in the back of a truck with a load of rubbish. So, seeing that there was no one round to ask, I hauled the lot out and lugged them home and put them in the front pond to rest until I had a hole dug. The previous lot I put in now have a tall bud.

More hollyhocks are up from the seeds I got hanging over a fence. I dreamt about hollyhocks last night. Perhaps because Hugh asked what they were and I didn't really succeed in explaining.

I have just heard the story (on the radio) of the Three Sisters that I see each day when I go for a walk – three very tall rocks towering over the Jamieson Valley. The story says that the three sisters were the object of desire of a tribe of Aborigines from Penrith. The Katoomba men wished to keep them in their tribe so a fight broke out. An old Katoomba man decided to protect the women by turning them into stone and planned, if the Katoomba men won the fight, to turn them back into women. The Katoomba men did win, but the old man died before he had a chance to return them to life. Their names were Mimi, Winmalee and Coomandoo.

These sisters keep their backs to me and face Katoomba no matter how I wish they would turn round. Perhaps they are still hoping Katoomba will return them to life. Longing, longing, longing.

Isn't it interesting how many of these stories from different cultures have the same basic themes. Women turned into swans, women sent to sleep by witches, and resurrection only because of some wonderful rescue by a man.

In the bath I saw a great blue-and-red rosella perched in the bird cherry eating the ripe red berries. I lay very quiet and still and watched it busily enjoying the fruit meant for it. Soon a group of green-and-red king parrots flew over to land there. I tasted the fruit, it is a little like a crab apple, juicy, tart and with a cherry flavour. I bet it would make a good jelly to have with meat. I am told the rowan berries that the birds are feasting on now make good jelly too. Sarah's tree has the debris from the berries under it just as if it was the last hour of a children's birthday party.

Last night as we sat under the cherry, a king parrot flew down and ate the cherries as we ate the chicken curry and pasta cake. The plum tree has dropped its fruit and before the birds get that I am going to make plum chutney.

I am reading *Sissinghurst, the making of a garden* by Anne Scott-James. V. Sackville West, as Vita liked to sign herself, also had a white garden. Hers was a theatre and mine is a teacosy. Her biography by Victoria Glendenning is one of the best things I've read in ages. How hard it is to find things to read that you can actually love. I lost the ability when I had Hugh and got a good dose of post-partum depression. Ever since then I've lost the knack of reading almost anything that turned up that was half-way decent. I am reading *Flaubert's Parrot* but I had to stop as it was D's and she's taken it home but will send it back when she's finished.

I'm also reading Angela Carter's *Sadean Women* but that, being about pornography, turned me pale and I had to go for a walk. It seems to me I know too much about men for my own good and I do not like attention drawn to it in books.

Luxury had its first review today. I was not at all displeased with it. Many critics simply can't resist showing off. They feel that if they say only favourable things the reader won't really respect them and so they add a quibble or two, or worse, pour on the vitriol mainly to show some fancy dancing. I am aware of a vast difference between ingratiators and cowards and the honest critics saying useful and insightful things in a stylish way. (Notice how many words are repeated in reviews, nearly all of them words I hate ... *perceptive, intelligent, evocative images* and so on. Very boring.) No, 'She writes like an angel with a feather dipped in a silver inkpot. I laughed, I cried, I damn near died. She mended my heart and went straight ahead and broke it'. And, 'I wanted to slit the throat of anyone who interrupted me while I was reading it'. That's the stuff I prefer. And listen to what Kafka says about writing: 'We need the books which affect us like a disaster ...' And, 'A book must be the axe, the icepick to the frozen sea in us'. Good, isn't it?

Tuesday, 4 February

It's sunny and I just turned round in this chair and saw the peaches are getting fatter so I'm off to see if they're ripe. No – cold, hard and unyielding. It will be March before I eat a peach here. They are ready in February in Adelaide, I remember. Everything is six weeks later here. As I am not speaking to myself, I will speak to you. The grass is wet and snails lie around anchored to the poison I threw down. They ate three hollyhock seedlings. Today there are fifteen growing in the herb pots at the bottom of the back stairs. I haven't seen a person since Sunday. No, I saw a woman in a raincoat yesterday from a distance disappearing in the mist down the street. I wonder if real life is passing me by. Why did I come here? I know the answer. I came because I fled. Flee down rat holes if you could, nothing leads back from the awful knowledge ... My worst thought is I might be wasting my life If sadness is the only lasting truth, then I'm not. Happiness, I tell myself, is always fleeting and ephemeral; doomed to vanish like a fog. Even today it's too late. 'Living, Postumus, is what the wise man did yesterday.' That's the Roman poet Martial. I suppose the only way I'll know if I've wasted my life is when I'm dying. 'Yes or no' I'll ask myself. 'Yes and no' I expect I'll reply.

I just picked up a book given to me years ago. It's a first edition of Yeats:

> We were the last romantics - chose for theme
> Traditional sanctity and loveliness;
> Whatever's written in what poets name
> The book of the people; whatever most can bless
> The mind of man or elevate a rhyme;
> But all is changed, that high horse riderless,
> Though mounted in that saddle Homer rode
> Where the swan drifts upon a darkening flood.

And the great irony is, I who have struggled so long and tried so hard to swear off romanticism am continually defeated by its glittering oils. All surface, they choke and kill and seduce like sirens. I even used John Tranter's words for the epigram in my first book.

Ah,
Romanticism! You give too little,
and take too much away.

And speaking of writing, the man who gave me the Yeats, John Robson, wrote to me about the strain of another kind of writing: 'As you say, academic writing is hard – I found myself, last Friday lunchtime, standing in David Jones' food hall, wobbly at the knees, bleary-eyed and light-headed, as I've never been for years – as a consequence of writing, that is.' (That's better.) 'I even think that some of the crankiness and at times downright insufferability of people like me is the result of the nervous drain of writing academic criticism year in, year out. I say *some* – you have to be a bit cranky to adopt such a life-style in the first place. People who've never done it would never believe it.'

And here's that Prince, Flaubert on the topic of academics:

I am now re-reading old Boileau, or rather I have been going through his complete works (just now I'm in the midst of his prose). He was a towering personality, and above all a great writer, much more than he was a poet. But how stupid he has been made out to be! What wretched interpreters and champions he has had! Professors – what a race! – pedants with pale ink! – they have lived off him and depleted him, *shredded* him, like a plague of beetles chewing the leaves off a tree. Not that he was all that tufty to begin with. No matter – his roots went deep, and he was upstanding, sturdy and solid ... At the moment I am mad about Juvenal. Such style! Such style!' (*September 30, 1853 to Louise Colet.*)

And now I am off to town with my green umbrella and fainting hope.

Friday, 7 February

Home again, home again, jiggety jig. I went to market and come home without a pig. Nor the bacon either, I admit. I did though get a nice red apple that seemed a good omen, fallen from a tree on to the path in Leichhardt. Lord, have I got debts. Still, while one lives, one has debts. Well, I do. It's no good wringing your hands madam, I tell myself, something must be done and quickly. But what. I don't know. I have just come in through the window, as Woolfie, who was here, left the key inside on the hall desk.

This morning I did a radio interview at Sydney University. Three young barefoot women were there, every chair was broken and one of the women had read two of my poems from the book she interviewed me about. It was very hot and there were graffiti on the walls, no fan, I had been lost half an hour trying to find the room. The microphone made a zinging sound and before that, the whole room was filled with a noise as if a tractor was starting. You write some poems and this is how you pay for it.

Sarah came as I was writing that and invited me to dinner. We sat in her dining-room and ate in the cool surrounded by oak furniture and floral curtains and blinds. Everyone here has floral curtains. It suits the place.

Saturday, 8 February
Cool, sunny and clear. When I got off the train from Sydney yesterday, the station felt like an old-fashioned cool room where country people keep their vegetables, flour and butter. The city was so hot no fan could cool my hot heart. I am at work, I am glad to report, on the galleys of the Penguin poetry book. It should be ready for release in July. Good. It's been three years in the doing. It feels like toffee in my hair. I love and hate this book.

I had lunch with Peri on her beautiful back verandah two days ago. Sitting in old white wicker chairs with blue cushions, an old Chinese wine table, and the orange cat asleep on the lawn, we talked about our trip to Adelaide for Writers' Week and the Festival.

Now I'm going to have a go at cabbages. I saw a photograph of one in today's paper and my mouth hungered for it. I am even prepared to put some in among the flowers. Like putting men and women together. Or say birds and animals. I think of men as elephants, different to us horses. Now I'm off to Snaps and to buy some seedlings.

Sunday, 9 February

Hot and windy. Rain may come at any time. The garden and I would welcome it. I have just picked a white gladiolus and put it in the bathroom. Small successes. Twenty hollyhocks are up. Knowing they will all be pink is a bit like knowing the sex of the baby you are about to have. Speaking of that, I bought a small jacket at an Animal Welfare League stall in the street yesterday for Kate Morven's boy she is about to have. It has small bright green apples for buttons. Maybe she's already had him, how would I know up here.

George brought my bicycle back yesterday afternoon. It has a new chain on it so I went for a ride this morning. It rinses my brain like a tub of blued rainwater. Do you remember knobs of blue? George stayed to dinner and then we watched Joan Sutherland in *Lucia di Lammermoor* with her red hair and tartan. We had a nice sauce for pasta that is made of mushrooms, anchovies and mint, fried in a little oil. It's good on toast or rice too.

On Friday on the train after staying with Mr Waterlily three days, I wrote a poem called *Pyromania*. Today I will type it. I have no ribbon in the typewriter so must type on to paper with carbon underneath. The blind typist.

At midnight when I walked out to see George off, the stars were so close. Through the blue peered a thousand pairs of foxes' eyes, lit by the hunter's spotlight. Blaze away. I long to see a shooting star. You already know what I'd wish. To shoot love straight between the eyes.

The Denisons have beaten me in the race to have a waterlily bloom. Theirs is out, pale yellow, they say. Soon I am going round to see it. I go out to my pond and say 'Bloom, lily, bloom', but it won't. Or can't.

Oh heavens it's hot. I splash water on my face at the kitchen sink and walk about sighing. My grandmother taught me to let cold water run over your wrists on hot days. It cools the body. Or it seems to. I think of her when I do it. So haughty with all that hair piled on like a gigantic silver beret. Mocking me behind the tray on her knees as she sat in bed. Ever the colonel's wife. She grew up in India and married my grandfather when he proposed to her over a bunch of Cecil Brunner roses. He was a little afraid of her too, like everyone else. He fought the Turks at Gallipoli and had to change his name to do it. Men wouldn't fight under a colonel with a German name, no matter how English he was. He had never been to Germany. His first name was Angelsey and his second, Siekman. He changed it to Brinkworth, which was his mother's maiden name. My father never got over it, and never spoke of it except to tell my mother, who told us. I think the shock of being Siekman Secundus at school one day and Brinkworth Secundus the next was too much for my shy father.

I think my father was hounded about this sudden change of name. He liked books and boats and sheep. He did not like fowls which my mother kept. Later on, he did however buy a chicken farm and made enough money to get a farm for each of my three brothers before he died. He didn't eat poultry. He wouldn't touch rabbit either, which he called 'underground mutton'. He sang love songs to my mother as he wiped the dishes. He said, putting his arm around her, 'Aren't cha lovely!' I watched. Yes, I admit it, I'm set like a frog in amber in my past.

The heat is laying the garden out like a boxer. I drink iced water and eat salad Niçoise. It is good in heat and there is no need to light the stove. An adaptation is just lettuce leaves, tomatoes, onion rings, olives, cucumber, green and red peppers, olive oil, tuna and boiled eggs, and cold boiled potatoes if you have them. I use eggs I pickled at Christmas time and with fresh bread and butter and lemon juice, no matter how hot it is this salad makes you eat.

Sometimes I think of writing as a game of cards played by one. You take out each word and lay it down. Some words, smart ones or favourite ones, are real aces, some are just small, two of diamonds, say, some are bleak and menacing as a nine of spades. It needs a steady hand and a calm eye and a face that reveals nothing and suddenly, lo, down goes a winning card and that paragraph or chapter is over. It's most especially like this in poetry.

I am reading John Boardman, *Athenian Black Figure Vases*. It's plain that many of these writers on classical matters are fine writers even though they are not necessarily setting out to make a work of art. I think there is a good reason for this, and it is that they studied ancient Greek. That language is really remarkable. It sounds like the sea and has as many moods. I tried to learn it at University but it was beyond me. I didn't even know what the English words meant when the elderly tall scholar said them. When he read us the death of Patroclus from *The Iliad*, tears rolled down his cheeks. He told me to keep on trying but I knew it was hopeless. I had no words for grammar. You need a word to do some things.

Here is Boardman in a sentence taken at random: 'Athenian vase painters of the middle of the seventh century could achieve a grandeur of scale and composition which the miniaturist black figure techniques of Corinth, although more controlled and precise, could not match.'

I'm having a look at this book because I think I have forgotten so much and I feel it is such an extravagant waste. When I was in Athens three years ago I stood in the Museum with thousands of pots, and realised with alarm I knew almost nothing about them though I'd spent so long learning. So, with a book as a butterfly net, I'm trying to recapture what I've lost.

Yesterday George filled my new fountain-pen with black ink I got at the newsagent that day. It is a treat to have this pen. Out of step with the times perhaps, everyone is buying word-processors or computers. (Perhaps they are the same thing.) George does not believe art can be judged good, better, worse or bad. Whenever I have thought something out and explored it enough in my mind I don't wish to discuss it with others. Because I like George, I talked with him about my art theories. I told him there are only two things in the world I really care about and they are art and love and I'm not sure that they are not the same thing. And that art is by its nature experimental. If people aren't interested in having experimental artists in their midst, they might remember if there hadn't been such artists, we'd still be back at the stage of the Greek pot as a way of depicting our society. Not that I mind Greek pots, as you know, but they do have their limitations. Once a Marxist literary critic and poet said to me, 'You do realise, don't you, that you are an elitist aesthete?' (Hurling this like a great rock over a wall at me.) I said I knew he meant that as an insult, but I took it as a compliment. Yes, it's true, I am guarding the gates against the tigers.

I admit my aesthetics are the product of the society I live in. So are everybody's. Western capitalist society, let's face it, has not made too bad a fist at making art. I place here the word Uffizzi and rest my case. Now fire away if you wish. I am off to water the garden.

Monday, 10 February
Thick white fog. A male bower bird was down drinking at the bird-bath when I went out to see the fog. A big golden-amber day lily is out. Next to the blue agapanthus it looks beautiful. What did last week accomplish? What will next week bring? Well, some progress on the Penguin book, the lawn was mowed, I wrote, that's about it. I think of Cicero whose maxim was exercise *mind* and *body*. Something for the mind every day, something for the body. Exercise the mind and body daily. In my own earnest way I try to.

There is an argument that goes like this, you may know it: 'The world is invented by language and we think in a language of words. There are only eight stories in the whole world and all tales use these in one form or another. People think in language. There can be no judgment about literature because it is all entirely subjective and the reader's relationship to the text is his and his alone and no judgment can be made regarding excellence or otherwise.' It drives me mad. It is based on Structuralism and post-Structuralism. What about those people who don't think in language? Is a composer thinking in language when he or she writes down the music they hear. If so, then music is a language. If music is a language, isn't painting too? Does a painter looking at an object he or she is painting or at the idea in the mind that is being painted, think in words or colour, texture and form? If they are thinking in form and so on, is painting a language? I have never sat inside any one else's brain, so I don't know what they do when they think but I *know* I think in images. When I want the answer to a problem, I pause and up surfaces an image like land coming out of a lake. It is an image that either describes the problem or the idea or it is a description of the answer. I use words to describe it later, but at that time it is simply visual.

None of this would bother me much if it weren't for the fact that the Structuralists are so utter about it. They base the whole theory about art on it and nothing else can be allowed. If you don't agree, they say it is because you don't understand.

Writing is about style and form. The form makes the style along with the content. For example, this journal is done in a style that came from the subject. You can't write about a garden in the same way you would write about your life if you were writing to your friends. The garden creates some formality in the writing. The rest has to go along with it or it would be too odd. So you end up writing about your friends and so on in a way you would not do otherwise.

The style was dictated by the form just as if form and content held a gun to my head. I had no choice.

Sarah has just called and we drove to Katoomba and I joined the library. I took a book about Kafka's letters, also a Paul Bowles novel, *Points in Time*. I took that because they had none of his wife's books there. He has a good reputation but she is very famous. Tennessee Williams thinks she is one of the greatest of this century.

One story I like about Jane Bowles is that being a drinker she often did odd things. A friend once saw her hail a taxi in Cairo, get in and walk straight out the other side. Now I think she may either have believed she had arrived, or she didn't like or trust the driver, or changed her mind. But it's the first that makes you laugh.

I also took out Katherine Mansfield's letters and journals.

Tuesday, 11 February
A wet foggy day, mild air and the apples dragging down the boughs. Green-and-red parrots in the bird cherry as I lay in the steaming bath watching them among the fog. Can there be anything better in this world than lying in a hot bath watching fog swirl through tree-tops while birds fly through like eye

~91~

motes. Not many, I think. I turn on the hot water with my big toe and gloat. Yesterday I did a lot on the galleys of the anthology and today I'll do more. It is really nearing its end. Like coming out of a terrible tunnel filled with spider webs and shrieks. I came close to cracking up over this book.

The plane tickets arrived yesterday for Writers' Week in Adelaide. I am planning what to say. I go on the twenty-seventh of this month and Peri is coming with me.

What fog. No need ever to drink here, things are so often hazy, painless, anaesthetised and mysterious. Birds call through the mist. It makes them sing. Someone rang from Melbourne and asked if that was birds she could hear. Yes.

Getting the milk I stood in the street simply hoping an on-coming car would see me. I realised that I was all in black apart from my green furled umbrella. Straight out of Jack the Ripper. Horses' hooves sound wonderful in it.

Two of my friends don't think very highly of Katherine Mansfield, because, they say, she uses so many words such as *pretty, little, beautiful* and so on. Female words they say. How daft. If you are stitching tapestry, you take tiny stitches. If you are a woman and wish to write as a woman, you use female language. Ernest Hemingway developed a style that entirely suited his content, his attitude and his views. So did she. [I]'... feel as fastidious as though I wrote with acid' she wrote to Middleton Murry in 1913.

Saturday, *15 February*

I went for a long walk down to the waterfalls and swam in the pool under the Lyrebird Dell waterfall. Yes, it was cold, but I felt so desperate with tiredness that I knew if I swam I'd recover. Just as I was about to strip off voices came down the hill. I waited while two small boys, their father and grand-mother passed. I didn't have a towel and went in in my under-wear, cursing the visitors. But later, as I climbed up the steps the father was coming down with wood for their fire and offer-ed his towel. I was dry enough so didn't take it, but the fact that I have met a local person doesn't displease me because I can see how isolated I have made myself and want to do something about it. I only know five people here and this after eight months.

As I walked home up the hot dusty track, a great black cockatoo flew out from some trees with his lemon feathered tail spread like a sail. Just before that a big red-and-blue parrot had flown out startled by my footsteps. I can't help it, they always seem like wonderful omens.

All along the track are bright blue berries on black stems bending under their weight springing out from dark green leaves of what I think must be a wild bulb. They look so poisonous, the colour is fierce like a plastic toy. It is berry and fruit time for the birds. Even the elm is covered in black berries or fruit, not unlike the bird cherry now that its fruit is going black with ripeness. I tasted the elm; it is like an olive but not as sour. The cherry is now even more like a real cherry. It would make liqueur, I think.

Sunday, 16 February
The sound of a big black currawong's wings flying past the window woke me. My first thought was what a lovely thing to be woken by, the sound of a bird flying. It is the opposite of getting out of bed on the wrong side. Five huge red-and-green parrots are in the top of the great pine I see from the kitchen window. How I long for binoculars. There is so much to eat at present the birds hardly touch what I throw out.

Peri has just rung. She's coming up to stay the night. Tomorrow she is taking me to *The Magic Flute* at the Opera House for my birthday present. Luciano Pavarotti is known here as Pav. We have named our favourite tenor after our favourite meringue.

Yesterday as I stood talking to Sarah who was lying sun-baking in her garden, a bird struck up like a solitary singer. We stopped and listened. Then she told me that a day or so before when it was grey and cloudy suddenly for half an hour the sun came out. The birds went mad and sang and sang. She said she almost joined in.

Wednesday, 19 February
Peri came and stayed. She arrived like an elegant white bird,

flower behind her ear. Each time she visits, I am happy. We walked to three waterfalls and I showed them off proud as a member of the landed gentry of his great stand of trees and breathtaking expanse of acres.

I went to town with Peri to *The Magic Flute*. No, we weren't very keen on it though we tried so hard to be. The Queen of the Night faltered like a horse on uneven ground, sank for a moment to the knees, and slowly and bravely raised her voice again to a more stable grip on her technique. It is heartrending to have to feel embarrassed for a singer and makes you feel resentful towards the person who has come to such grief.

I stayed at Leichhardt and spent the usual time torn between dementia and ecstacy.

I've just done my Matron's round of the garden and now can write in this report that the camellias have many buds sprouting their tiny green hands towards winter. They are one of the few plants looking forward to winter. I can't say I am. It is the days and days of fog that I find rigorous. Not being able to see out for several days has a queer effect and gets very claustrophobic, even to the edge of a desperate white panic. That's when I leap on a train and flee to town for a few days. The wood fires are nice though, the garden open with the green gone, and the birds glad of any food.

A friend wrote from Canberra the sort of letter every writer reads with a straightening of the back, a most grateful smile and a drop more courage in the heart. She is a painter and I stayed with her and her husband in Vienna. I had been so lonely, having spent three months at that stage mainly alone in Europe, that to talk to an artist in English about our work was water in the desert. She took me round the city day after day showing me the architecture and telling me the history. I was tired of art museums by then so cafés and buildings and her company were just what I needed.

An Australian musician came to dinner and gave me a ticket to the opera he was conducting and so had a spare ticket. After dinner we walked past Beethoven's house. That's Vienna for you. Music, madness, suicides, architecture, art and history, side by side like letters in a word that spells Vienna. I went to the

Café Lautmann to write in the evening. It is where the Nazi officers used to meet to have coffee. Their Headquarters were across the road. I did it to test my nerve. It's like writing in the tomb of a murdered person.

I've just come back from the three waterfall walk and I'm whistling. Lord I love this place. No amount of isolation or lonely nights is too much to pay. A big parrot with bright blue tail and wings and a back that was crimson flew out of some ti-trees. I crept up and away he flew again like love. Skinks, lizards and geckos are lying on the paths sunning themselves on old dry gum leaves like surfers on their boards. They skitter off when they see your shadow or hear your step.

When Peri and I walked we saw a pink-and-grey galah feeding young in the hollow trunk of an enormous snow gum. The mate sat watching on a branch of a gum a few feet away.

After lunch today I lay in the sun reading some books to find a few last-minute replacement poems for the anthology as there's been a slight hitch. A big bird cherry was blowing in the wind with its green branches almost on the ground swinging like a hooped skirt. The wind is up and all along the paths on the walk bark lies in strips. When I got out of the train in a sleeveless silk blouse, the wind blew over my chest like a methylated spirit rub. The Village Storekeeper said it had been blowing and howling all night. But here, away from the heights, it's sheltered and less windy.

The hitch to the anthology that I mentioned is, I might admit, rather more than that. At this late stage with the galleys in our hands I feel fairly murderous.

Outside the moon pours light in the shape of a crucifix. I stared through the glass in the window, lifted it and sure enough, the cross was still there. I ran outside to watch. No, it was just a refraction of the light through the wire of the window screen. It was so exactly like the star you see in children's religious books leading the Kings to the stable or above the shepherds as they gaze up with their crooks and flocks. Were they all looking through a wire screen, and if not, how did the painters invent that image.

Thursday, 20 February
Now the sun pours down like manna. Gordon and Woolfie's last day here. They arrived late last night and leave for Greece tonight. No longer will the tracks be tramped by these two red-haired women and the tall thin man. Well, not for a year anyway.

We have just been for a walk with George to Bridal Veil Falls and down to an amphitheatre halfway to the floor of the valley. Down through tree-ferns, water and small dells with the water always running beside you wanting you to come *this way, this way,* urgently like a faerie. Bridal Veil Falls is a great veil of water falling over a wide tall rock hundreds of metres high with a frill of white water running down the edge. The Father of the bride stands taller, unveiled, beside it is a gigantic rock in the sun beside the bride.

Down, then, with glimpses of the mountains retreating away like an army that never ends. We sat in the amphitheatre puffing a bit and had some claret and apple pie, with Gordon and Woolfie wondering at times why they were leaving. We had lunch here under the tree and now George is asleep in the hammock and Gordon is packing and Woolfie has gone round to the Denisons to photocopy her manuscript.

Friday, 21 February
One sniff and autumn is here. It has come in the air like an invisible red brown and yellow bird. It is sitting near the apples so red and green saying 'Quick, quick, quick, winter's coming'. It is absolutely my favourite time of the year. It is the saddest too. Autumn grieves. Winter says 'I am', Spring says 'Here I am' and Summer says 'Let's enjoy each other'. So, I suppose Autumn is sad because it's the end of an affair.

What a good day. I am halfway through the anthology's biographies. Virtue has added a sheen to my skin. I am wearing my mother's pink crêpe-de-chine honeymoon nightdress. In this nightdress I sleep as if drugged. My parents left their honeymoon hotel when they became bored and went to stay with friends. Ever afterwards my Aunty Eileen told the story of how she found the sash of this garment in the bottom of their bed.

My father dealt with this family joke by actually, it seemed to me, becoming invisible.

On the top of every tree tonight there are birds calling up the rain from the grey clouds assembling like an audience for a great rock concert.

Oh goodnight. Off I go, polishing my halo with the hem of my nightdress.

Saturday, 22 February
It's getting hot. Sarah and I walked down to Snaps this morning. Seven pink-and-grey galahs flew over as we talked about our schemes for work. We walked into the store and bought our spinach, parsley, milk and so on. I'm living on the smell of an oily rag, as they say, and not unhappy to do it either. The reason is there's an immense difference between people who have chosen to live with little money and those who are condemned to it.

Today I finished the biographies. An immense relief. I have just walked outside and saw I was standing in a cloud. Coming indoors I realised this journal has become like a lover who takes time away from work. A secret vice. An illicit passion. There's never anything more delicious.

Sunday, 23 February
Wet apples. Big silver drops are hanging on the red and green apples. As I lay listening to some music in the back sunroom, a big king parrot flew down to a branch of the young gum close by. His back was moss green, with a red head and breast. His beak was red too. The back was like a cloak worn by some boy king in a South American jungle. Then five more flew down and sat swaying and nodding in the mist.

Sarah and I went for a walk before lunch in a deep fog. Water dripping off the pines, the air muffled in its silent scarf of fog and through this, birds call.

David Denison is back from Los Angeles. He flew there for a week on Pan Am's last flight out of Australia. He seems unruffled by it, though it was his first overseas trip. In a minute I'm going round to have a coffee with them to say goodbye before I leave for Adelaide.

I stay at Mr Waterlily's for a few days to do some last-minute business on the anthology before I go.

At the Denisons' waiting for them to come home from a walk I went round their garden, resting and wet like a horse hosed after a race. Lydia came in and said that today walking here at Leura is like being inside a mother of pearl shell. People say the most wonderful things. Peri said, looking at the mountains covered with gums that they were like broccoli. Jean said, walking home past Leuralla's ancient pines, they were like busbies on soldiers in the sky. Each time I walk all these friends travel with me because I see their images as I pass.

Wednesday, 26 February

Now my journal travels with me. Tomorrow early in the morning we are flying to Adelaide.

Yesterday I had lunch in Peri's garden with an author. They were examining old embroideries that Peri has collected and our friend plans to use in her book on Australian women's crafts for the Bicentennial Year Celebrations. Quilts, handstitched, covered in butterflies, Peri's daughter's names embroidered in the centre of each quilt, given to them as they turned twenty-one. As we ate we talked about all the things we could remember our mothers doing. Nostalgia pulled up a chair and got stuck into the pasta, wine and salad. Unaware, eyes on other things, we grew up while these women toiled away and now we turn and stare and think of all we missed.

~ 7 ~

March

Welcome to Writers' Week. It's over forty degrees or 100°
fahrenheit. People melt like candles in a wind. Today I sat in
one of the tents by the Torrens River, and with four other
Australian poets read to people lying backwards in their chairs
fanning themselves with programmes. They looked like actors
in a European avant-garde drama. Stiff, backward leaning and
bizarre with the shock of the heat.

I sleep in Angela's study and lie on a futon watching the birds
land in two young gums. One is so erotic. A bare pink trunk like
an English callgirl's leg out of which sprout two branches like
upward arms. It is lemon-scented.

Last night on the *Popeye* ... my what a beginning to a sentence.
Could be the start of a novel. On the dark river, with pelicans
drifting near the reeds, five poets read to about sixty people.
Throb, throb goes the engine when the boatman turns it off and
we glide down the river like a heavy swan. It is the most dif-
ficult place I have ever read. A small light, a boat moving
beneath your feet, a microphone to hold and a button to keep
pressed. Suddenly that terrible bird of nervousness perched on
my shoulder and would not go away. My hand trembled, I had
difficulty in not allowing my voice to tremble, and in the end, I
hung on to a pole with one hand, held my book in the other and
a woman held the microphone for me. I could have wept with
fury at myself for having that happen. There is as far as I know
nothing you can do when that bird lands. Just hang on and try to
get through. I'm told it wasn't really noticeable but I am not so
sure. Today in the tent was better, it was even fun, and I told
them a story first and then read and enjoyed it hugely. I am a
real show off.

Connie and Peri are at *Voss* the new Australian opera and
Angela and I are waiting for them to come home. Mr Waterlily
has just rung up and I did my usual joking phone talk to him. He

loves me to make him laugh but unfortunately he doesn't love me as far as I can tell. No he can't love me, let's face it, because if he did he wouldn't have another woman would he? Polygamy for men, monogamy for women, what's new? And here am I, pure as the driven snow, so far, through no fault of my own, I confess. To quote Dorothy Hewett: 'My capacity for faithfulness was always limited.' And if you think that is some kind of tortured logic, let me explain. There is one thing on this earth I long for almost as much as wanting to want nothing, and that is mutual fidelity. It is elusive as a greased eel and no matter how long I stare into the gloomy waters of the pond, stretch out my arms foolishly trying to grasp it, it always slips away even when I feel I have it at last in my grip.

Saturday, 8 March
Yesterday at the blue-and-red striped marquee, I listened to a man say he thought women had, on the whole, been overpraised for their work here in recent years. I think there may be something in it. But oh, how these cocks crow when for so long in small ways we have had to assert our places on the perch. The history of writing is paved with heaps of men who have been overpraised. We hear no apologies about that. Enough.

Today is cooler, the pink garden umbrella is half-opened like a new mushroom with the climbing white Star of Bethlehem on the lattice behind. The pink chrysanthemums are blooming and above them jacarandas in full ferny leaf are drooping.

Every day I go to the Festival bistro and have lunch by the river, slow and dark green. I had lunch with two novelists yesterday and was so nervous as I cut my steak I put down my fork and knew I couldn't eat it. I fancy one of them. When I poured the wine I missed the glass by about five inches. Today Peri is driving to Hahndorf with her daughter Sheridan. I am going to the last part of Writers' Week, the lunch at an old pub in North Adelaide. Grapevines trailing overhead and beneath that some pounding hearts and high hopes.

Later
What a horrid lunch. Only the desperate, mad, drunk, and sad. Places sometimes just get worn out. This is a threadbare sheet.

Some of the guests looked as if they'd been on drug rehabilitation programmes and a few as if it hadn't been at all successful. My best talk was with a disturbed person on the footpath while I waited for the taxi. He seemed sanest. The more upset you become the more the disturbed seem rational and wise. If this keeps on I'll end up speaking in tongues. I want to go camping. I've just been to *Voss* with Connie. The desert at night with stars and peace that's what I want. Bed, bed, oh, my holy bed.

Monday, 10 March
Here are three birds stained like flames eating the flowers of the pink-trunked gum. There is a method of making Easter eggs that gives the same effect as their feathers. I made them for my brothers but could never wait until Easter Sunday to give them out, so Good Friday was always the day they got their eggs. Blow hen's eggs, cut crêpe paper into one-inch squares, dip it in water and stick it all around the egg in various and many colours, wrap it in cloth until it dries, out comes an egg stained like a window in church. Fabergé to my eyes never made anything lovelier.

Behind the gum with these birds, two seagulls flew in front of a cream and pale grey cloud just as if they were from a different film. Everything was silent.

Peri and I have just come back from a visit to an old friend at Henley Beach. The sea was long and stretched to the horizon as if it had been flattened by a rolling-pin. Fifty different blues with white-topped waves and into that stretched the jetty like an ancient crone's warning finger. The Queen tried to disembark here from a boat but it was too rough and she had to go away.

Peri has brought home a box of freshly picked strawberries from Hahndorf, sweeter and stronger than any strawberry I ever had.

Oh, and I almost forgot, the best sight I saw today was a flock of seagulls at the beach, flapping like a crocheted cloth against the blue sky. A lace cloth made of birds. All crying to be unravelled.

Tuesday, 11 March
I dreamt twice of Iceland poppies. A great patch of them
blowing on a hillside and I was sitting beside them. What can it
mean? Poppies, I suppose. Then I dreamt I planted four punnets
of them in my garden. What can that mean? Plant poppies, I
suppose. I certainly will the moment I get home.

Yesterday at a fair with Peri I bought wind chimes for my
verandah. They sound like bells and are Chinese lacquer red
and made of long pieces of tubular steel and wood.

No one is up yet. It is very quiet. The trees outside this study
are very still standing waiting for the birds like mothers for
their children coming home. On a stobie pole is the biggest
black, black crow I've ever seen. It is eating something and using
the wooden cross of the pole as a table. South Australians are
nicknamed Crow Eaters. It's probably true that people did once
eat them. The pioneers had little choice if the boat didn't
arrive or the crop failed. And now we dine on strawberries (and
even shark's lips the other night at dinner).

At the Burnside pool the hundred-year-old gums hold blue
birds, yes, truly. Bright green parrots fly over like emeralds
flung upwards. I swim with my head out and smile and stare.
The bottom of the pool has never interested me.

I went to see the Awaji puppets. They are bright figures three-
quarters lifesize, with bad pasts. All the evil of the damaged
psyche drags behind them in the form of black-dressed
puppeteers crawling round to manipulate them. Shudder to see
your life on stage.

Wednesday, 12 March
Autumn is ringing the doorbell and I have a nervous tic in my
eye. It is cool and the air smells of apples.

Yesterday Peri and I drove to Gawler for lunch with my
mother. She had made a floral carpet and a photogapher was
there to take pictures for the book on Australian women's crafts.
My mother had used gumnut buds and the flower of the ivy with
Michelmas daisies and purple statice to make the carpet. It
took almost ten hours and as she made it, the ivy flowers were
changing colour from the heat. It was on a small table on the

front lawn with the young woman taking photos and my mother beside it holding a bunch of blue flowers plucked from the hedge to make her image look better. I blinked to stop feeling anything. Walking down Rundle Street as a young woman, my mother used to buy flowers that matched her frock to carry in her hands.

Friday, 14 March
Hot and torrid. The weather is hot, the pace the other. Today we are driving to the Barossa Valley to a pheasant farm for lunch.

Yesterday at an Italian grocer's on Norwood Parade Peri took photographs of the huge display of cheeses and olives. As we were driving away in the small apple-green Volkswagen Peri has hired, I saw a swag of green quinces hanging over a wall. I told Peri and she pulled up and backed to the tree. There we saw a small gum with acid-yellow flowers and burnt red gumnut buds. The smell was straight from every Australian schoolyard's memory. I can smell it now and know the old dry sandy road at Tumby Bay with the scent pouring out in the heat and the sound of a few bees or maybe blowflies, and it is lunch time and I am walking home to lunch with my friend Heather Bell. Our cool houses are darkened by blinds to keep out the heat. Soon we will have to hurry past the shop on our way back to school with an orange or perhaps some leaves to draw for the afternoon class. Outside the shop was a man exposing himself to us as we rushed past his awful silence. I often thought it was a sleepy lizard he had falling out of his trousers and then later it seemed this great white *something* that should not be there. We had no words for this and told no one. We did not even speak of it to each other.

Instead we told each other wonderful stories. I hoped she believed me and I knew I should believe her. I was a heroine, daring and notable, everyone was full of praise. I was clever, top girl, very beloved. In my tales, my mother sang my praises to the world. I had a nervous feeling sometimes that Heather might have a suspicion I was lying on a gigantic scale. Her tales were more modest, and for all I know, may have been true.

Back behind our desks, safe at last, only the Headmaster and his ruler to fear, we drew the oranges or the gum leaves next to a water glass and tried to get the eliptical curve of the lip of the glass to match the praise we so ardently wished for from the eliptical lips of our teacher with her grey bun and wild ways.

Saturday, 15 March
Peri has just gone home. She drove off with the old green VW laden with jams (from my mother's kitchen), small trees of every type she had admired here, cheeses from the Italian grocery, a vast jar of antipasto - slices of peppers, artichokes, carrots, mushrooms and so on, like a painting, a full-size ceramic pumpkin, a red handknitted coat she found in a craft shop and a case that would barely close. A satisfied woman. Lugging home the loot.

Yesterday we had lunch beside a small lake where trout and tortoises lived with old white gums and reeds. This was the pheasant farm restaurant set in the vineyards of the Barossa near the Seppeltsfield winery with its thousands of palm trees planted in avenues that stretch for miles. It could have been Yugoslavia. Breast of pheasant with juniper berries and mashed pumpkin, red fried beetroot and green beans is a good dish.

After the trip to the grocery where jars are sold for homemade wine, we pulled up at a nursery to buy trees. At the house opposite an Italian man and woman were standing on ladders, a white cotton scarf over the the woman's hair, secateurs in hands, buckets on elbows, harvesting the vine over their drive. Over their fence hung orange persimmons, green olives thick as grapes, a cumquat tree and in the garden next door, a big pomegranate with red fruit like hanging lanterns. We almost applauded. All this fruitfulness and opulence is so easily worn, it is so casual, so taken for granted and so beautiful.

At the nursery we showed the red and yellow flowering gum flowers we'd picked in Norwood and they sold us some of those trees as well as five pink-trunked gums. I bought a cement kitsch plaque with a garden poem on it. I could barely lift it and when Mr Waterlily meets the plane his face will be a stern study and

I shall laugh. I have five jars of fig jam, trusty typewriter, books, manuscripts, table linen from my mother, an old photograph album and a big suitcase of clothes.

Sunday, 16 March
I have just been for a walk with my friend Marisa round the Torrens. Wild duck, ibis and water hens floated past or stood on the bank near the reeds. Above were grey-trunked gums and willows. We walked the hanging bridge while local boys were jumping on the end to make it shake. Not looking down, I stumbled on straight ahead swallowing my panic. Marisa and her husband Philip made a cold Italian lunch underneath their grapevine. We picked five different leaves from the herb garden with small red tomatoes in a silver colander and ate it with vitello tonnato, a lemon pith salad, bread and Italian wine. For this lemon salad you need one or two very large lemons with a lot of pith. Peel the lemons. The pith is cut in chunks and dressed with olive oil and parsley. It must be eaten at once.

Monday, 17 March
Tonight I fly home. It is early morning and the only noise is the water of the shower and the birds. A crow is calling. It is the sound of every farm on hot mornings. I went to see my friend's son play Macbeth in a youth theatre show. As the whole play was done on straw and they simply tossed it up for battle scenes, I have been sneezing ever since. Afterwards, saying goodbye to my friend, the Adelaide casino queue was stretching away with its eager hopes and an Italian man was saying his rosary silently with busy desperate fingers as he waited. It looked tragic.

And now, after lunch, I say goodbye to my friends. Angela and Connie ask if I'll miss all this and the answer is strangely, no. The truth is I can't afford to. Even when Woolfie left to go with Gordon for a year to live in Greece, I walked into my bedroom and thought 'Am I going to cry?' The answer was no. I just don't look back. There's something very tough in me. I am never afraid of burglars, if I was, I couldn't live alone fearlessly. I am a very practical woman. I appear hard. Perhaps I am. I am a survivor.

Goodbye, Adelaide. I have painted my nails bright pink and want to be razzle-dazzle on my way out.

Tuesday, 19 March
Home to red windfallen apples. I did Matron's round of the garden, picked one pink rose, saw that nothing has been lost, thanks to the Denisons doing some watering, and the weeds are feeling very optimistic. Cleaning out the fridge as I am now, and weeding, are jobs that make me feel somehow poisoned at the feast. If I'd had an apron on I'd have gathered the apples in the skirt as women have for centuries. I want to make chutney from them. So pretty, the colour of ripe pomegranates.

I swept the paths where the birds have dropped cherries and torn-off small branches, began unpacking, put the cement poem under the apricot tree like a small tombstone, read the mail, and swallowed at the awful bills with their red stickers and messages that mean 'We hate you'.

Now to get the gas turned back on. I'm sure I don't need to elaborate on why it has been turned off.

This garden needs so much done to it, our affair has come to a bit of a slump. I have a game I play in which I say all the plants and trees I'd like to buy over to myself until I say an *um* or an *er*. For example: 'Four white magnolias, ten peonies, three Japanese maples, thirty silver birches, twenty tulips, fifty daffodils, ten blue iris, two punnets of poppies, two of pansies, two of cinerarias, three clematis, ten roses, white and yellow, one climbing Peace rose, *ummmm*. Out ...'

The waterlily in the pond has not had a flower, nor do I think it ever will. I was met at the airport and stayed at Leichhardt overnight. We have a Jekyll and Hyde affair. All night we act like children running on a beach, happy, innocent, beautiful from love. As the sun comes up we grow disturbed, unpredictable, insecure, frightened, weird, nervous, like a nasty-tempered horse.

The chimes I bought in Adelaide are hung on the verandah and a little gust has sung ding-dong. They have a sound like church bells. I think that's because they're made of steel.

I have just been down to the escarpment in the dusk with the

Three Sisters there like bishops, tall, stately, still, in the cathedral. I called in on Sarah who, like me, is finding the daylight-saving difficult to adjust to. I wanted dinner at four o'clock today, so naturally, having, as my mother says, no one to please but myself, I had it. Now for the holy bath and the sacred bed. Amen, home again.

Wednesday, 20 March
As I watched the fog spreading through the garden, it looked so like smoke in the heat I sniffed unconsciously then walked towards it and stood while it swirled around like dry ice in the theatre. I have been round to see the Denisons and to collect my post from them. After I'd told them the news and gossip from Adelaide I asked what had been happening. David said, 'We've done the big bed and the cat's had kittens'. The big bed means a new curving bed they have cut out from the lawn and planted with old-fashioned roses and many different kinds of small plants. Lydia showed it to me with a bird-bath under a birch tree with grasses planted around the bath and behind that some small spikey iris to give more shape and height. Imagine being able to answer a 'what's been happening' question in that way. They have struggled hard for this peace, I know.

Beside Lydia's studio a bed of lavender-pink coloured crocus are out. Behind them are Japanese ranunculi waving hundreds of pink flowers. Truly if Monet walked in even he would be impressed. Monet's garden is my favourite. Perfect to my eye because it is simply full of flowers and I am mad on flowers.

I just went out to water the garden and a magpie was there on the lawn lifting its beak to the sky singing the marvellous song as if it poured like water down its trembling throat. Bower birds are back. Even though a few returned a month or so ago as I said, no more came, but today in Sarah's bird cherry, five flew round and above them, red-and-green parrots.

Truly this is heaven's zoo.

Thursday, 21 March
Pulling out petunias. A full wheelbarrow standing by an empty bed. I got a lot of weeds too and feel very smug. I can never pull

up a weed without hearing Mr Waterlily telling me: 'Always remember that the definition of a weed is something that *likes* to be disturbed.' In other words, get the roots out too. That will stay with me for ever.

Two dishes of pansies and petunia heads are here beside me plucked as it were from the jaws of death. There will be no more till Spring and heaven knows (and how I long to) what will have happened by then ...

When I got back from Adelaide there was an offer waiting from a publisher and that was a real pleasure to read. I am thinking it over and not sure what to do just yet, so as always, I am doing nothing. Many things solve themselves I think and need not be acted on at all. Haste is often messy and disruptive, though it seems crucial at the time.

My own compost at last. I have just put a barrow of it round some of the roses. They look so drab and I said to Lydia and David last evening as we walked round my garden that it was obvious they needed manure and spray. Lydia asked why and I said because their leaves were falling off. She pointed out that it was normal and, in fact, they were only sticks, if I remembered, when I bought them. Of course she's right but I put the compost round as the soil looks so arid and poor lately. Where, oh, where is someone who will bring me a load of free manure? I would cook for a week for that one.

I have just put an advertisement to share this house in the *Sydney Morning Herald*. I have procrastinated for ages because I am worried I might attract someone a bit nutty, or worse. However, I have so far had a guardian angel. All round Europe it was hard-pressed but brought me safely home.

Speaking of Europe, where are Gordon and Woolfie? Not a word since they left.

Halley's Comet is coming over here and David says at five in the morning from my back deck I should be able to see it. Many people are coming to the mountains to see it. I told David I was glad I would not be here to see it again and he replied that he felt the same. Too much pain, he said. What on earth is wrong with us, set in Eden with spears in our hearts.

Saturday, 22 March
One of the nicest things I know is grilled kidneys on pitta bread. Half-cook the kidneys, then put them on top of the bread so that it catches the juices. Return the kidneys on the bread to the griller to finish cooking. Before serving, toss oregano on to them. (The simplest dishes are the most difficult to describe). This is eaten with lemon juice and a salad with a green garlic dressing, pepper and a glass of wine.

I wrote a long poem late last night and nearly dropped off to sleep in Snaps this morning. I have this minute decided to enter it in the Mattara contest as that prize-money may save my brass candlesticks from the bailiffs.

Sunday, 23 March
Haunted houses. I don't believe in them but Sarah took me to see a beautiful Victorian house with pressed tin walls and paintings done in the panels under a bay window made of pale pink and lemon stained-glass. The owner was in the garden gathering lavender, wearing a pink Liberty print frock. The Mitchell Library is sending a photographer next week to record the paintings which were painted over once but are now cleaned. It is like separating a curtain and stepping back into the past century. Any moment a man with muttonchop whiskers will appear saying: 'And where the hell's my breakfast? What do we keep Annie for if she can't get a meal ready on time? She's not the same since she got knocked up; whoever managed that!' (He did.) And the wife, hurrying round apologising and saying, 'Annie won't be long dear'. (Nor will the child, and when she sees the red hair she just might put two and two together. Then life with an unfaithful man will give her a true and rigorous training for hell.)

I've been at this typewriter almost five hours now and it's a marvellous day so I'm off for a walk.

Monday, 24 March
Every night Halley's Comet sails past and I sleep on. Last night I was determined to try to wake. The radio gave a time for the appearance: four-forty a.m. I went to sleep telling myself to

wake at that time. I woke, looked at my watch, a miracle! Exactly four-forty. I ran out, no comet. Inside I looked again at the watch and saw I'd looked at it upside down. Eleven-ten makes four-forty precisely. Perhaps I'll book an early-morning telephone call for tomorrow.

I woke up today, forced my eyes open and the light streaming in between the gap in the thick white curtains fell into my mind like the contents of a fridge.

I have advertised this house to share. Even the woman who took the advertisement said it sounded so nice she'd like to drop out and come up. I told her she'd be welcome. Now I must stay near the phone.

The four gums I brought back from Adelaide went in today. Two pink-trunked ones are in among the jasmine hedge and may they not be choked. I put a tree fertiliser pellet in with each tree, looked up to see they had a clear sky to reach, watered them and left them to it. Tree planting makes me quite frenzied. I got some cinerarias, half-dead, from the florist to plant when it's cooler.

Thursday, 27 March
I've let this house to a policeman. I expect to feel very safe. For two days I've been in the city to get material for the Christina Stead biography. Today before I got the train home I swam at Balmoral. At its most perfect, that sweet beach stretching between the two headlands of the bay is like a favourite featherbed, the like of which are only found in the homes of German grandmothers or in small hotels in Germany. I had one in Wiesbaden and one at Angaston in the Barossa Valley in South Australia. The blue flat sea stretches out like a quilt with silver sparkles. I am happy at Balmoral.

I have been thinking about cooking because friends are coming for Easter. I see now I have left two kilos of lamb chops on the train so the dish I am making with the biggest most beautiful eggplants I ever saw will have to be eaten with something else.

Easter is the time to be in Greece. In a hotel dining-room, a few tables set near the bar looking out over the blue caldera of the distance to the volcano at Santorini, I met two young Athenians.

The man came up to me and told me they had no soap in their room. I said that it was a pity, but I didn't see what I could do about it. He apologised and said he thought I was a chamber-maid. Do I look so Greek?

Yanni was an engineer who had worked in Manchester for seven years and Tati was an architect who had no English at all and had just graduated from the University of Athens. She wore headphones and listened to Greek music while he talked to me, as I think only Greeks can. Philosophy, politics, gossip, and history poured from his lips in that blend of English that only someone with the history of Homer seems capable of using.

On Yanni's big BMW motor-bike the three of us cruised round the mountain curves of that island, laughing, cracking jokes. Tati, earphones off, had the jokes translated by her boyfriend. When we stopped we drank ouzo, ate at tiny tavernas and my appetite for once was matched by hers. We sunbaked on rocky beaches, swam in those salty blue waters, explored small villages where at noon all the inhabitants withdrew indoors and slept and we, like the last mortals, walked around under our straw hats looking at whole towns painted in a miracle of communal art in only blue and green against the white blazing whitewash.

Tati and I rode donkeys up the switchback track of the Santor-ini cliff, she holding her hat and screeching in Greek, I bellow-ing to the donkeyman to stop hitting the poor donkey that, with the others, bled from the blows and left the trail in spots in the dust all the days of their awful life. Yanni walked on laughing.

One day we hired a small boat and went to another island. Out in the open bay a wind came up with waves as high as the mast. Three Greek women, Tati and I clutched each other and screamed in a contagion of most enjoyable terror while the boatman steered and Yanni said that truly, the sea would not capsize us. We anchored near a beach and waded ashore, had a swim and went into a small taverna perched on some rocks. In the one big room that held tables and chairs, the stove, a cook and a waitress, a vast ancient double bed sat, made up ready for their rest whenever they needed it, or customers were not about, or the sun went down.

We ate Greek yogurt, tiny grilled fish, salad, tsadziki, kid, crusty white bread and drank retsina.

The first English word Yanni taught Tati was 'Aesthetics'. I have often thought about that.

On their last night we went for a ride after dinner where we sat at blue-and-white cement tables eating small dried octopus that hung on a washing-line across the tables. Calling for 'more wine, Adonia' (who was ten and earning money with her eleven-year-old sister Aphrodite) while Yorggos the owner, sipping wine, turned the meat, chicken and fish on the barbecue until all were fed. Then if it was a Festival, and that was about once a week, he danced with his mother, she all in black holding a white handkerchief, linking her to the other dancers a quarter of her age while his father, propped on his walking stick like a boat against the wall, watched and was occasionally and most tenderly led off to the lavatory by his wife.

Yanni, Tati and I swung through towns and past vineyards and the low fields of tomatoes for which Santorini is famous. A flat tyre put a halt to that. It was in a town, about one o'clock in the morning, no one on the whole island had any method of fixing a tyre. We propped ourselves up on chairs outside a closed café and waited until dawn when a taxi took us to our hotel. Greek men have been known to have explosive tempers, but to his eternal credit, not one cross word came from Yanni though he had a contract to fulfil in Athens in two days. Finally I lent him drachmas and they got the bike to the ferry with the help of a garage man. When I arrived in Athens a week or so later, I rang Yanni. He arrived on the red bike and said we would go to lunch and it would be a surprise. We had lunch at a taverna by the sea and before our first bite or sip he put on the table the money I had lent them.

Ah, Yanni and Tati, where are you now? Is that wild Greek music still blaring out from your earphones Tati, while you smile at a conversation of which you understand not one word, never showing a jealous or impatient quibble? And Yanni, are you still haring round Athens on that bike in all the cacophony, fumes and ghastliness? Still tearing off to Poseidon's temple taking the curves you love so well with Tati on the back, looking happy, vague and silent, eating local sweets each time she gets a chance and never growing stout? *Evcharisto* you two and hello.

Friday, 28 March
Good Friday. Surely the world's saddest music is played on the radio on Good Friday. I could sob into the bread I am kneading.

To calm a sad mind, cooking comes close to gardening. Salsa verde, in a version that bears little resemblance except the name to the original, bread, hot cross buns, vichyssoise, roast leg of hogget, sweet potatoes baked with pumpkin and white onion sauce are all either on, done, or about to be made. If cooking calms me, I should be almost unconscious.

I am considering old-fashioned lemon pudding. D is coming and if I don't make it she asks for it. Over the years, of all the things I've made for guests, it's been the thing I think perhaps they have enjoyed most. And it's probably one of the easiest. I don't actually have a recipe. It's true and accurate version is in the old Green and Gold Cookery Book put out by the mothers of the boys at Kings College, Adelaide, in about 1940. But this is how I do it. Melt about a cup of margarine or butter in a pan, add a cup of sugar, juice and rind of two lemons and two cups of milk. Beat all, then add three beaten egg yolks and one tablespoon of plain flour. Fold in stiffly beaten egg whites. Bake in a pan of hot water in a heatproof dish in the oven at moderate heat for about thirty minutes, or less if the top is browning. Serve with cream. It is runny with a golden crust.

Saturday, 29 March
Easter Saturday. At last, news from Paris of Gordon and Woolfie who are now engaged with an 1847 engagement ring of coral and pearl to prove it. Old-fashioned ring, for an old-fashioned thing. On their way to Crete. Sad, ugly, poor, beautiful, brave Crete.

Monday, 31 March
Easter Monday. The satin bower bird is back. As I began to write Jean called out saying she thought perhaps the male bower bird

had arrived. I ran out and there he was, slimmer, darker in the damp air than I remembered him from last winter. Andrew, D, Jean and I stood like statues in the sunroom looking out at a big group of female and young green bower birds and this loopy blue hot-shot ink-drop male.

Yesterday we walked to the waterfalls with a basket of sausages, bread and wine and some dry sticks in a bag. We cooked the sausages in foil as there was nothing else there to hold them and now there is a new method in my cuisine for barbecues with neither hot plates nor grillers. We sat in the cave at Lyrebird Dell and drank the wine and laughed.

At Wentworth Falls, a garden was open to the public and we drove there in Jean's car. A lake with a blue, purple, lavender and lemon-painted bridge across it holds a weeping willow, the reflection of a pink fish-kite hanging from a tree and the calmness only water can bring. Great pines have hundreds and hundreds of azaleas under them and beyond that lawns green and curving take you round beds and up small hills to more things you long to see. Then you go home very quietly affected by what your eye drank in.

Craig End came to dinner and the four of us described the three best and worst plays we have seen in the last decade. Craig told of a student production where Jove hung by accident from the flies, upside down above the proscenium arch and shouting, delivered half his lines, until the machinery righted itself and he was thrown across the stage still shouting. The audience laughed so much they had to drop the curtain and call for quiet. I told of *Aida* where, standing singing alone, *Aida* took off her crown and the wig came with it. Bald as a badger, she sang her lungs out for another five minutes.

We have just walked round under an umbrella each to the Denisons' garden. There, trees dripping with water, the curving low stone walls slowly being covered with flowering creepers, the summer-house, damp and childish like a playhouse on a rainy day. D had a swing under the great pine. The red carp were swimming around a cream waterlily bud.

Soon I must go to town with Jean and do I wish to do it, no I don't. But appointments must be kept and business done.

~ 8 ~

April

Wednesday, 2 April

'I will lift up mine eyes to the hills ...' I always think of that when I walk from the train down the Mall to my house. Receding down the street are layers of tree tops and then the blue mountains stretching layer on layer like a crinkled blue filo pastry. Today it is hot with a clear blue sky arching over it all. Laden with food from the shop and a rejected manuscript and clothes I took to the city, I walked home feeling like a soldier on a forced march watching the way my strength increased as the trip went on and nearer my home I drew.

I am cheerful today, not sure why, plenty of reasons to be worried but it doesn't seem necessary. I ring the wind chimes as I walk in and out and feel pleased with the world against all odds. Love? That falls on you like a breath of angels, fades and returns and goes with the regularity of the moon.

Now I will go out and throw bread around the lawn to see if I can entice back the blue eye of heaven, that male bower bird.

Thursday, 3 April

I hung the hammock in the hot air. George came and drank coffee beside it while I lay swinging, trailing one foot to keep swaying with little pushes on the lawn.

I haven't been able to use my typewriter until now because men have been working on the electricity lines. No radio makes things so quiet. I go out and ring my chimes from time to time if I'm lonely. I must struggle not to become eccentric.

I do not wish to report what has happened to the waterlily in the front pond, but I will. It has only one leaf left. Something ate it or it gave up hope. Perhaps it was in too much shadow.

A long letter from Woolfie in Paris. Still on their way to Crete. They sit in bars and make up stories about the people there. She wishes to live in Paris. Who doesn't?

Also, the *Herald* wrote to say that the computer ate my poem.

After four months of looking each Saturday for this thing of mine, I now hear it has perished. However ... I have a copy and they will get it first thing as soon as I can stagger up the Mall to the post office. One door closes and another slams in your face.

The white garden is not doing well – too much shade.

Once I made an all-white meal and asked ten friends to come dressed in white. The room had green-and-white wallpaper and black chairs upholstered in white leather. The meal was terrible. Iced cucumber soup before chicken in white sauce with cauliflower and mashed potatoes and a cucumber and onion salad, I think. (Could I really have gone that far?) Then something like floating island pudding which is custard with poached meringues on top. One friend, a sculptor, defied me and wore all black and that was best of all among the whiteness.

Now it's night time and I have been out looking for Halley's Comet. I have searched the sky. No luck. The chiffon scarf of the milky way is flung across the sky as if some happy reckless goddess careened there in her chariot, trailing it gathering stars as sequins. I walked down to the corner in my dressing-gown but still couldn't find it. In a car's headlights I probably looked like someone running away from hospital.

Friday, 4 April
A fire ban has been declared. A drought has been declared. I put on my straw hat and walked to the post office with the letters I have written chasing lost, or perhaps, dead poets for the anthology. We should have their written permission, or that of their executors, before we can go to print. Their letters have come back 'return to sender'. One or two I think have gone governessing on some outback station.

I am making ratatouille to freeze for winter. Perhaps it is my German ancestry coming out. When I feel the first breeze change to that autumn snap like the crack of a whip when I go out to empty the tea-leaves in the morning, I have a great urge to start preserving. It is some ancient ancestral memory of cellars full of sausages and kegs of sauerkraut and the knowledge: *we will get through this terrible winter.*

Back to the ratatouille and my secret vice, boiled cabbage

with caraway seeds and butter. How odd to crave that on this hot day.

Before I come back to this journal I hope like mad to have seen Halley's Comet. George is coming to take me for a drink and to see a film at a film fesitval. He knows where the Comet is and he has a telescope too.

Saturday, 5 April
No, George and I didn't find the Comet. Long we craned to the sky like geese sensing foxes. Just the Southern Cross, the Milky Way, but no Comet trailing its train of promises, or threats.

The policeman who is to share this house moves in next Thursday. He won't have a gun, I asked him. I told him I'm a pacifist because that's the truth, and he said he will be working for an insurance company without a gun. He is hanging up his uniform, belt and all. He is engaged to a nurse.

Sunday, 6 April
The Comet! The Comet! Well, at least I think it was. A low fuzz above the guttering. I feel like singing with Peggy Lee ... 'Is that all there is?' Are all my blinding lights to turn out to be low fuzzes? People, I'm told, have come from all over the world to see it Some Japanese were placated by being taught to throw boomerangs in a park. I saw this on television.

The fire is lit, the cauliflower cheese is in the oven, the fish is waiting and Mr Waterlily, who doesn't deserve all this, is coming to lunch.

Tuesday, 8 April
Hi diddle diddle, the cat and the fiddle ... that's me singing. I have been to town. Yes, I am singing and smiling. The birds are fed, the garden watered and if all is not quite right with my world, it is as near as may be.

One of the forty azaleas I brought up here from the city last winter is almost dead. I saw it wilting on Sunday, but too stupid from love, walked away. Now I see the situation is critical. I've often tinkered with the thought that plants may be screaming and I not hearing. I was told the reason there is only one leaf left on the waterlily is that the level of water is too low. So the pond is now full and as water always has seemed to me the other word for love, may it thrive and bloom even yet. Well, perhaps not bloom, but at least get a few leaves and perhaps a pale bud before the frost.

Wednesday, 9 April

Rats. I have rats. I must get a trap. They roll apples round the floor at night. The blue bowl is half-emptied of its apples and the rest have pieces taken.

There are eleven bower birds in the garden eating rice. Big ones, smaller ones, all burnished copper green. No male in sight. Today I must work, work, work.

I long for aquasol, it's the garden equivalent of egg flips for poorly children. Mine were reared on egg flips and fish soup. Hugh once complained to a friend that he was reared on bones. He meant the bones of soups.

It is not the things you know you got wrong with your children that they are likely to complain of later, it is the things you thought you got right. Accused of sloth, untidiness, loose morals, bad company, drink, iced-up refrigerators, I would have only agreed. But the food, I thought, was all right. I tired them of cakes and biscuits by baking and offering them so many. Now they don't eat cake. All the rest was what hundreds who came, ate and said was good. That is my defence. I rest my case. Also, before I go, how is it that they are so tall and well, if the food was so bad? Genetics aren't everything you know, Your Honour.

Today I saw a whole new area of Leura. A piece of my mail was sent to the wrong address and because it was vital (*vital?* the Penguin book merely hangs on it) I walked miles to inquire after it. I met an elderly woman who asked if I lived in a house with a brown picket fence. I said I did. She told me she had given my son and his girlfriend a lift at Christmas time and, she said: 'The girl was carrying a bunch of lilies.' (Those Madonna lilies scented my house for days.) The woman showed me round her garden. She has hundreds of self-sewn small Japanese maples ready to dig up and transplant. They are already three years old she says and here, people put their mower over them. So, if you want Japanese maples, go where they grow and ask for seedlings. This is called country life.

When I got home the currawongs were singing a hymn of praise because of the food I had put out. A black-faced shrike came down to eat too. On Sunday we saw gang gang cockatoos and a flock of black cockatoos flying over the pines.

Today there was a partial eclipse of the sun. On Saturday night there will be an eclipse of the moon. Saturn is visible and its rings too, with the help of a small telescope, I hear. Tomorrow the Comet will come closest to earth. Riddled as I am with superstition, these truly seem harbingers of yes, good news. If *only* I could get a good look at one of them.

David said, after I told him I'd seen a certain fuzziness that was the Comet, that if I saw the Star of Bethlehem, I'd have arrived at the manger saying: 'What's this fuzz?'

Thursday, 10 April
Oh, have you seen this day? Eve woke up the first morning in Eden and saw this day. I swear the air has spice in it. Today I buy a rat trap. Today, too, is the day the policeman comes to live here. Oh, and may it be easy and happy.

Poppies, poppies. I have planted two punnets. And, like the Polish bartender at the Opera House, I brewed the best martinis I was capable of for all the plants. Buckets of blue-green aerosol. I sat drinking those cocktails at that bar one day with a man to whom I was to say goodbye in a few hours.

Friday, 11 April
Another '*Have* you seen this *day*?' As when Adam woke in Eden, looked around on that first day, and saw that it was good. I have been feeding the birds and my new lodger, like me, stands staring out as the light streams through the pines. The policeman arrived with a trailer full of tools. In half an hour we had hung all the paintings in the study, nailed up Gordon and Woolfie's tea-chests, fixed the falling wallpaper and carried in a large bookshelf. I unpacked the boxes of books which had been sitting waiting since I arrived, and lo, the room was done. How much energy people get from each other.

By the end of the day I had weeded the lawn, shopped, gardened, stored files, unpacked from Adelaide ... what, not unpacked yet? Well, I am now.

Some punnets of dying poppies and pansies I have seen in a shop keep coming to my mind. It's like seeing a truck of sheep standing in the sun moaning. There are two new varieties of pansies there too, one is burgundy and looks as if it had a Spanish grandmother. One has a pink edge. I'm tempted. Does a gambler seeing a roulette wheel feel like this? It is called obsession. Where's my hat. I'm off. Call me the Mother Teresa of poppies and pansies. I'm coming my darlings, I'm coming.

'Well,' she says, taking off her hat, wiping her brow and unleashing her stays, 'that's four punnets sprung from the jaws of death.' And now safely home and in their beds these happy plants sit under a moon about, they say, to be eclipsed while their unhappy fellows wilt in that Gestapo chamber of horrors called a shop.

The policeman has set two mouse traps with melon seeds. Does he think these rats are from Greece? One is gentle. I see it's got the seed without the crash. I expect a bang any second from the other. Today he cut ten or so lowest branches from the pines to let light on to the plants below. The white lilacs are in light they haven't seen since they left the nursery, and the foxgloves are free to really get going about their business.

So what if Mr Waterlily chooses to go to the country this weekend with another, so what if Caroline has rung to say she isn't coming. I am busy with my plants and am dry-eyed and swaggering ... swagger ... swagger ...

Saturday, 12 April

The blue angel is back. Hopping round the lawn on his yellow legs, this blue bird that always seems to arrive like a consolation hurled from the sky. He is much less brave than his wives, only coming to earth for a minute or two after they have been on the lawn before him. Then they all eat the bread and turn it into flight and song.

A fog has come and to announce it every bird is singing its throat out.

Tonight the eclipse of the moon but with the cloud, fog and my present mood, I think bed is better than staring and hoping.

Sunday, 13 April
I have been for a walk to Olympian Rock. Laid out before me, the valley, the mountains, the Three Sisters, the shadows of the clouds on the cliffs and the sea of trees, and above all this an eagle like a god's wink.

Before the walk, I had coffee at the Denisons. David took some photos in the garden because he has a new camera. They have planted wallflowers in the new curved bed, with pansies, old-fashioned roses and many other things.

Because my grandmother was German and grew wallflowers, and there had been a war, I thought they were called war flowers.

Monday, 14 April
I have news. Good and bad, sad and happy. I have ended the affair. In the country, when dogs or other animals are mortally ill, the farmer takes a gun. Well, as Eve Arden said in *All About Eve*, 'Here's to the men we've loved ... the stinkers'. No, I'm not bitter, merely resigned. In fact, optimism surges through me in small waves.

It's as if a very old frail person lying in a hospital bed decided to cut the thin thread in the night. Drifted off, and in the morning, people saw, sighed but knew it was inevitable and merely something to accept with as much grace as can be found.

Now I am off to town.

You could say the prison door was always open and finally I have decided to walk through it. So Mr Waterlily will stalk these pages no longer and a good thing too. When to stay is as painful as to go, you might as well go, as one day it will be painful no longer.

Wednesday, 16 April
Home, a sunny day and the poppy plants waving. The azalea I forget to water, will, perhaps, live. It is called Pink Dream. I brush it squatting beside it, to get off the dead leaves and

~121~

encourage it as if it was unconscious in hospital. Don't give up. Don't give up.

I came home on an afternoon train yesterday and Sarah came to dinner. Craig End's first episode of a television serial was on so we watched and rang him afterwards. He's now employed to write other episodes.

I keep thinking of the colour yellow. It is full of hope and I wave it like a flag in my mind. Yellow flags for the faint of heart.

I have been sitting in the sun on the verandah sorting out the Penguin permissions letters. Nine lost poets to find and then the book can go ahead.

I am reading Jung's *Memories, Dreams, Reflections*. As ever, the very thing I need is put into my hand by a friend. This book is so calm, so wise, and so conscious of our roots, I see myself as simply a part of a process. I was asked recently 'What do you really want?' At first I said: 'To be loved'. Then I said: 'No, what I really want is to want nothing, but does that only come like a ticket with death?' In the end, I suppose, it comes to wishing for peace and acceptance without, however, resignation. I want to go to my grave without resignation. That seems like bowing as if beaten. Acceptance is more equal and gracious. Like taking fate as a gift.

I was looking at a photograph of Jung by Cartier-Bresson and saw how the hands of old people are like gloves. Then I thought of the people I walk past at the geriatric hospital every day in their chairs anchored by their gravity and the slow loss of movement and saw that they wear their bodies like gloves. As if the body was preparing to be sloughed off like a snake skin and just the spirit left to float free.

Thursday, 17 April
Grey storms are coming. The pines are groaning in the wind and the birds are excited. Some olive green, red and blue parrots are swooping round the garden and perching in the pine branches lying on the lawn. I must get a bird book.

Light the fire, make chicken soup and walk to the post office after putting things in envelopes.

Doors are banging, the chimes are ringing. I feel quite odd and even, if I allow it, happy.

The dogwood trees are turning colour. Here, now are the promised bracts of colour on the leaves. They are rose pink and green, very beautiful. That word *bracts* again. How I love it. I could sniff it like a rose.

Friday, 18 April

Autumn, sun, a windy day and leaves stained like a sunset in the wind. I have been for a long walk. Some streets are lined with ornamental cherry trees turned red and behind them trees gone yellow as wheat. The mountains stretch away like a blue promise of a calm infinity.

When I got home I pulled out at least ten weeds. Then I ripped off a few handsful of agapanthus leaves that were shading the cinerarias and came inside puffing with a hearty pleasure of at least having struck a blow or two. Perhaps I haven't really got the character for becoming a gardener. We will see.

A gardener I met on a walk told me two useful things. One was that maples and dogwood have matted surface roots and cannot be dug near and so are no good near annuals. The other was advice to plant ground cover. He hasn't seen my garden but says I need more ground cover. He is right. There are about thirty metres of blue alphine phlox in his garden and they must be one of the most beautiful covers a garden can wear. I told this gardener, so calm, so rooted like a tree there on his plot, that I read Edna Walling. He replied that his sister, in 1920, gave him a book of hers and he's been using her philosophy ever since.

And tonight a half moon with a cross of light glowing like a benediction through the bedroom window.

Saturday, 19 April

Such a day. Sun streaming through the window on to the pillows as it does only in autumn and winter. When I came here the sun was doing this, and now it has begun again. I lie and sunbake with the papers and a cup of tea, for the hour it pours in. Flat as a lizard. Sarah has booked to go riding tomorrow. I will walk because I don't ride and that is final. No correspondence will be entered into.

Hugh and Emily are coming for the weekend.

Sunday, 20 April

And so they did. And now have gone. After breakfast we walked to the waterfalls and as he has ever since he could walk, Hugh turned over rocks in pools looking for creatures. He found a big red-and-blue yabby with babies under a rock. Then, satisfied, he put the yabby back and covered it with bark. Once he told me recently that it is his dream to drain every ocean, look, and then put all the water back. From the age of three where there was water he asked over and over 'How deep is it? 'Never a pond, lake, sea, creek, dam, river or pool did we see but that I estimated its depth at his urgent request.

At Medlow Bath, Sarah was shown a small black brumby mare that she plans to ride. It was found here in the bush, the owner said, and has a bridle but nothing else on its frightened skin. I walked around and asked the price of manure. It is free but Sarah wouldn't let me put it in her car because of the smell.

We had a barbecue on the escarpment and that miracle that is supposed to happen, but doesn't always, occurred. The burnt, charred sausages were more delicious than larks' tongues; the chops, sublime and smoky; the salad, as I always try to make it, but seldom succeed; the chutney, the perfect match for the smoky flavours, and the moselle the very thing. We lay in the sun faces to the blue sky half-asleep, hands behind our heads and felt we might never rise again.

For the first time I saw gang gang cockatoos close up. Four of these rare beauties were eating berries, happy, busy and merging in and out of the shade and leaves and light like dancers through green veils. They have bright pink heads and grey bodies with beautiful striped breasts, flecked with black or brown.

This afternoon as I lay reading when everyone had gone home, I read the word *Sad*. I could not make it out. I kept thinking it was *Sadt* or *Satd*. Is this because I will not admit the word because I am fighting hard against its meaning?

Monday, 21 April

As I sat down to write I caught a piece of the curtains, and struggling to release it wrenched the rod from the wall. Down came curtain rings, rod and all. Now there is a hole in the wall.

I have been out pulling up jasmine and honeysuckle that is choking my neighbour's ground covers. There is no fence between us so I feel responsible. These creepers have gone yards into the garden and the strawberry cover and the campanula and the violets are almost hidden. All this happened without me noticing it. Like life, big changes can take place in a garden utterly unnoticed until almost too late.

The sky is a blue glass dome over us all and where the pine trees reach almost to the top, four great black cockatoos flew over screaming as I feel sure Icarus did before he landed. And when Icarus jumped off that cliff in Crete watched by his anxious father Dædalus, did he before he fell headlong into the sea, as the wax melted on his wings, realize that he was simply one more young man hell bent on outdoing Dad? And with that, the waters closed over his beautiful head, and Crete sank back in a swoon like a mother.

Speaking of Crete, Woolfie, I hear, has either not gone there or has left and is in London in hospital with a broken jaw because a door slammed in her face. No address for her, no word, so my letters pile up at the post office in Chania. Perhaps it is merely rumour and at this moment she is out sailing across the blue Aegean, pointing to the birds above with Gordon, smiling and silent beside her. I think not, somehow.

I see now I was wrong about Icarus. He wasn't exactly trying to outdo his father, merely go as far as him in their flight to Sicily. I just looked it up in the Classical Dictionary. Did you know that Dædalus invented the folding chair, among other things? And he gave the thread to Ariadne for Theseus. He devised the cow disguise for Queen Parsiphæ and was imprisoned with Icarus by King Minos for this crime. Having invented the labyrinth for the Minotaur, it was just another challenge to invent wings ... and he and Icarus were flying out when the boy went too near the sun. However, Dædalus arrived safely in Sicily. I imagine he carefully folded up the wings and put them in a box ready for any other emergency. Nobody loves a smarty, and as any inventor or artist will tell you, there is nothing jealous people won't do when they fear you. Ironically, no one would have know this better than Dædalus himself, because he killed his own nephew, Perdix, whose skill was greater than his own.

Jung says jealousy comes from lack of love. I have been thinking about that but some people seem more jealous than others. It is as if they have an insatiable appetite for love. As with plants and water, do some people need more love than others?

It was because of Queen Parsiphæ's liaison with the bull that the Minotaur was born and therein began the tale of the maze, the flight and the fall.

Like so many things from the ancient Greeks, it all seems so modern. Here's the cautionary word to scientists, those who help to invent monsters bear the consequences in undreamt-of ways. And if that's not modern, I don't know what is.

I am trying to practise the Chinese dinner method. The method relates to a story a friend of mine who is a potter once told me. He ate a ten-course Chinese banquet in a restaurant one night. At each course, he wondered what the next would be and so on, until at the end of the meal, he realised he hadn't tasted anything, so lost in anticipation was he. Instead of longing for love, fidelity, intimacy and trust, and so on, all those exquisite luxuries that are supposed to be available in return for the same, I am now trying to live in the moment. It is not exactly easy but I feel it is a worthwhile exercise. I have no wish to wake up on my death bed thinking of waste. I am determined to try to avoid sadness wafting over a life like a scent. No, it will not do. I am screwing down the cap firmly on that bottle. Let's try a bit of dignity and enjoyment. Dab a bit behind each ear and on the wrists.

Slashing away again as the jasmine I kept thinking of my favourite of all politicians, Cicero. I have been doing the Ciceronic thing, exercising the mind and the body daily. A garden achieves all that. The eye is pleased. And to achieve this, the body has to work, work, work. To learn what will grow, and where and when to plant it, to design the garden to be the thing of harmony and sighs that you hope for, to know the names and idiosyncrasies of the trees and plants, all this can't help but exercise the mind.

I am going to town because a friend has a show of paintings opening tomorrow night.

Saturday, 26 April

All night the wind has rung the chimes. A handmaiden sent by the weather, the wind gently undresses the trees like brides for their wedding night with winter who, at this moment, is walking down the corridor.

I have been out feeding my flock. The currawongs come now as soon as they hear me call. There is whistling, calling, chirping, singing, every bird sound except the screeching of the black cockatoos, and over that, a counter tenor singing a Renaissance song on the radio.

Monday, 28 April

'What is death but a failure of the heart.' (Dorothy Hewitt.) All the wheels came off my cart today. I lay in bed and couldn't act. I had been so busy dancing to keep the tigers at bay, and suddenly I could move no more. I rang Sarah and she came and gave me a cup of tea and some normal human talk with the sun pouring in on her blonde hair as she sat on my bed. I must, must get over this. My affair is over and I want to heal, but instead lie weakly waiting for a miracle.

Tuesday, 29 April

Outside the trees are shouting, gold, red and pink with arms raised as if they are about to dance. Indoors the mood is more sober.

I did not want to drink this cup. I held it in my hand for months, turning my face away knowing it must be done. And now it is and I lie gasping and sobbing, dreaming of Socrates. He, at least, made no fuss but simply said: 'Down the hatch,' as he tossed it off, then lay back prepared to die as his friends watched weeping.

'To every thing there is a season, and a time to every purpose under the heaven: A time to be born, and a time to die; a time to plant, and a time to pluck at that which is planted; a time to kill, and a time to heal; a time to break down, and a time to build up; a time to weep, and a time to laugh; a time to mourn and a time to dance ...' Well, this is a time I do not like a scrap but it must be passed through, so onwards through the tunnel I must go.

When the sun comes out, I am going to take photographs of autumn before it goes home, takes off its ballgown and lies down under winter's pall.

It's now dusk and all day the fog has swept slowly round the house like a drape of veil until the house is turbanned now like a dowager. It needs one vast amethyst stuck over the front door to resemble an Edith Sitwell costume. Pin that on and then, perhaps, the house will begin to recite long poems to the trees. All day I've staggered around like a poisoned horse. It seems strange, but not uncommon, how one's legs go from under one when the mind's in pain. And yet, and yet, I feel optimistic. This will pass. And in the passing, peace and a modicum of self-respect will grow, I hope. Pious hopes! The fact is I am wretched and simply wish to groan.

Wednesday, 30 April
All night it's rained. I thought the sound was mice playing in the kitchen. I went out after ages listening and it was the gutters overflowing. Now inside the earth the bulbs must be feeling this, the icy kiss of winter and its wife the rain. Soon they will stir and I will run out every morning with my cup of tea to count the green heads shooting. Matron counting the babies in her nursery. That my dressing-gown is white adds to the effect.

Today I go to teach at Milperra.

~ 128 ~

~ 9 ~

May

Friday, 2 May

Last night Andrew Grafton came to stay and George came to dinner too. They are old friends. Caroline and her boyfriend Jim are coming tonight to stay, so I am defrosting the leg of hogget because they don't get much meat being students in Newtown.

I am watching myself heal myself with interest. The body heals, as a rule, whether it is the mind inside or the flesh, and that seems so miraculous. Beautiful surroundings help. Jean Rhys stuck it out in bedsitters and always seemed to keep a grip on herself, and had humour and her sentences that I love so much. This is nothing like that ... outside the autumn going mad like the last stages of a party with balloons, frenzied dancing and music that you never want to end. Inside my white room the sun streaming in and a maple at the window like a red banner.

The cinerarias are definitely getting bigger and even the foxgloves and hollyhocks are larger now. Life seems to lie between the hopes and the action, something to do with lighting the fire, drinking tea and having a conversation with a friend. John Lennon said: 'Life is what happens while you're making other plans.'

The miracle I have longed for is going to happen in the usual unexpected way. I am recovering. Possibly rudely soon. But I can't see the point of suffering simply out of politeness. Now where are my boot straps, I must give them another hitch ...

Fire in the mist. The trees like flames are shooting through the fog. The difference between this and a bushfire is that it is cold and wet here. A surreal dream of summer.

The washing is drying by the fire, the day is almost over, and, as in all recoveries, even that feels an achievement. I was thinking as I lay on the bed after a nap that it is not an unusual or remarkable thing that one more man has been spreading his seed among the women's tears with a ruthless and concerned agony. When I think that I feel ashamed to weep.

I have just called a taxi to collect Caroline and Jim from the train as it is raining. I love country living. The driver knows not only where I live, but who owned the house before me. I said that she is twenty, blonde with a blond boyfriend and will be carrying bags. That is enough, the driver will find them. Now to make lemon pudding.

Saturday, 3 May
Two fair children tucked up in each other's arms. Over twenty currawongs flew down like a troupe of harvesters as I threw out cold potatoes. Currawongs simply love cooked potatoes. They swoop down when I call and throw out potatoes. Some just gobble and some peck delicately as invalids. Perhaps they have personalities. Why not? It seems every other creature has. I am unbalancing nature. Currawongs I'm told chase off the other birds. You interfere in other people's lives to their peril and so too with birds.

Yesterday Andrew and I went out in the afternoon and gathered big branches of autumn leaves and berries. I am set to decorate St Albyn's church for a wedding today. Half the night I thought of leaves and ribbons and tossed and turned. I want it to look absolutely wonderful. If I could, I'd drag a tree in. I want swags of berries, branches of cherries, bowls of chrysanthemums and sighs of joy from the guests. I will have to be satisfied with something less than this, naturally.

Now three female bower birds have flown down. Where is the male, the glimpse of blue hope I long to see.

Sunday, 4 May
The church is done, and I pronounce it good. Andrew, Caroline, Jim and Sarah came to help me. Caroline standing, branches in hand, halfway up the aisle said: 'I hate churches, they give me the creeps.' I asked if she'd just shove those agapanthus green heads into the vase and put the berries in the altar vase. She said: 'Am I annoying you?' I explained I was tired, worried, cold and wanted to get it done and make some lunch at home and would talk about these political and philosophical matters later. Young Marxists decorating a church could take all day.

Put the things in vases and go home to lunch, the fire, the wine and a rest, I say.

Today I am pleased with the wild bowls of autumn, never did I see bowls that pleased me more. It is a curious thing even to me why I cared so much. Later Sarah and I went down and watched the bride go in to marry. We peered down the aisle and will probably appear like two ancient unknown sibyls in every photograph. I hope we don't bring her bad luck, we seemed so like crones in a Greek chorus.

At dusk Andrew and I walked to Leura cascades as the mist blew around parts of the valley and above the mountains a pink dusk changed the clouds and light. The ferns and bushes were covered in raindrops and when the light fell down everything sparkled like crystals on green strings. I got a big armful of amber leaves of cherry and red maple and berries for this house. Lauren Bacall and Mr Bogart, as she calls him, were on television in *To Have and Have Not*. We watched and ate cheese and apples.

Caroline and Jim left this morning and when I asked if it was for a meeting or a demonstration, Jim told me it is May Day, so it is the march.

Andrew and I have read some of our new poems and planned a few things. Winning a prize or two and writing a work of art and other such not so easy tasks. I had a phone call; an English voice asking if I'd like a visitor. It was my friend Mary whose grandmother was a friend of my grandmother, and whose mother was a friend of my mother, and who was my friend in a country town and whose children met my children when she took hers across the Nullabor Plain. She has been here three months grape-picking on the River Murray. After twenty-five years in England she has come home to stay. So, as Andrew was leaving, Mary arrived and here we have sat by the fire talking. She has come to stay a while, enjoying at present the bath after months in a tent in the heat.

And Andrew has left a poem about hogget and eating and walking and talking and wine drinking and sleeping at my house. It is a Gertrude Stein style poem and I am very pleased to have it. Shall I say in similar fashion that it is now clear to me it is all visitors coming and going and then being alone and then visitors and cooking and cups of tea and talking and then picnics and looking at the vast blue valley and the fire and the autumn, and then meals and making dinners and breakfasts and then looking at the plants and feeding the birds and stoking up the fire and writing in between. Something like that.

Monday, 5 May
Amused, tolerant, detatched, that is how Mary decided at ten she wished to live her life. And so it is. Me, I keep jumping off cliffs with only a coathanger and screaming all the way down to the floor of the valley. I really wish to stop doing this and before it is too late, want to find another way to live. Meanwhile, in between these leaps, my life goes on.

Wednesday, 7 May
Autumn is screaming silently and we go about our business nodding and sighing, defeated, unable to do anything to save it or describe its silent astonishing turmoil. Mary is out taking photographs. I am dyeing things black. Only because they will look modern; there's no symbolism to it (for once).

At dusk yesterday I took Mary to see the waterfalls with the fog swirling through the valley. After hundreds of kilometres of driving over plains, these mountains are a shock to her. I never knew anyone who loved the Australian landscape more. Yet she has spent twenty-five years in Dorset, married to an Englishman. Homesick. Now she has come home to stay. Thank God.

I did a round of the garden this morning and saw that since we had rain a few days ago, the cinerarias are almost double in size and the pansies pushing away at their business of growing fast before the cold.

I scanned the places where the bulbs lie. Underneath, they are stirring like a foetus the moment before the heartbeat begins. Who can hear the first heartbeat, who can say the hour it begins, who can tell anything of these except the moment the mother feels the first stirring in her womb or the gardener sees a shoot.

I've made watercress soup. It is easy and good and one of my favourite things. We got watercress in Katoomba when Mary and I went there on Monday. If you wish to make it, fry two or three potatoes and an onion in butter, don't let that get brown, but add some chicken stock or water and cook until it's tender. Add a big handful or two of watercress, cleaned, washed and chopped. Cook for a minute or so. Put into a blender with two cups of cold milk and some uncooked watercress, chopped up to make it a prettier green. Serve hot or cold.

Thursday, 8 May
I rang George and said Mary and I were walking to Bridal Veil Falls and invited him. He came within the hour, an action I like so much, no ifs and maybe's, just, 'Yes, I'll be there'. We took some food and wine in rucksacks and climbed down and then up and then down with birds calling and us puffing and talking. Round the corner of a cliff set in the sun a million years ago we sat on a bit of moss and ate sandwiches, some blue cheese, hard-boiled eggs, and apples. Then we drank the wine, or did we do that before or during? Yes, and we walked home with legs trembling from the steps and more stopping and looking at views was done to secretly pause for breath than was done on the way there. On the cliff we had a talk about mathematics and poetry that I enjoyed although no real conclusions were required, but that is the type of talk I like very much. Those who wish to be right and prove you wrong have never interested me in the long run. I prefer juggling to throwing and catching.

Woolfie has written from Crete and they are all right and off to Yugoslavia with no forwarding address. I have overcome this by writing to them and not posting the letters. I will send them off when I get an address and that way I feel calmer and not defeated by having to wait. (As a child I used to write the end of episodes in comic books that were serials to be continued. That way I knew the end and it was one I liked.)

Friday, 9 May
Mulch. I have been tossing and turning thinking of oak leaves and ashes. Today is the day for Mary and me to go down my lane

with the wheelbarrow, get the oak leaves, fallen like old love letters left from a dead affairs, strew them on the roses and cover them with ashes from the fireplace.

We went to the escarpment and got a load of gum sticks for kindling. Tying the load down with our sweaters, gardening gloves on top, it was a long way from the ballroom and long white kid gloves where we once danced the modern waltz in strapless tafetta dresses. That was when we were meant to get our husbands whom we later ditched. Or did they ditch us? A bit of both probably. Anyway, we singularly failed to please. We, who were bred for little else. Now we dig and cut and gather talking theories and laughing a bit from time to time.

Right now Mary is cutting winter wood for me and 'rationalising', as she puts it, the place under the house where it is kept. The thudding and thumping are changing it from a dump to a tidy woodpile and I am glad. Thin as a rail, tough as wire from the three months grape-picking (four tons before lunch she says). I see I have made her sound like a fence.

Sunday, 11 May
Grey gang gang cockatoos came past screaming like fighter planes as I was kneeling down taking a photograph of the woodheap Mary designed in graduating sizes of logs. We put out some bird seed to encourage the sparrows and the parrots. Mary reared a sparrow fallen from the nest in England, she told me, as we stood watching a small flock on the lawn. It was bald, blind and yet never soiled the cotton wool nest she made for it in her kitchen. She fed it by chewing Bengers Food and putting it down its throat with eyebrow tweezers. It liked to sit on shoulders and nestle into hair and naturally did not know it was not a person for a long time. Sparrows hearing it call came anxiously to her sill and flew away defeated, over and over again. It grew feathers, opened its eyes, learned to fly as she threw it into the air and perched on a branch of a pear tree stuck in a pot in the kitchen. One day it flew off as a flock of sparrows flew over and joined them. Now beat that for a successful story.

George has just called in and talked over the plans for the long walk to the Blue Gum Forest we plan tomorrow. He has taken a long rope from Mary's camping gear. We surmise it is to help us cross a river. I am not well and not sure I can do this trek but don't want to back out.

The Jim Smith book on the Blue Mountains and the trails is stern in warnings; idle, indolent and casual as I am with a hearty penchant for eating on walks and turning them into parties, I am nervous of this trip. Nervous yet ardent, that's me.

Hugh has come to stay and last night we went to dinner at a new restaurant at Katoomba. He told Mary and me about the boat trip he has just done on the Hawkesbury River with Emily. They got oysters from rocks and caught big blue swimmer crabs that they cooked and ate dangling their legs from the back of the boat and throwing the shells into the water. They caught flounder and bream from lines and cat fish and ate those too. A boy and a girl, a motor cruiser, some fishing lines and five days to play.

Australia, not only The Lucky Country, but the world's best-kept secret.

Monday, 12 May
Today is the day for the trek to the Blue Gum Forest. I can't go because I'm sick. Drat and damn. My chest feels as if I ate some barbed wire.

It is an interesting and salutary thing to see that when you refuse to fill the role someone wishes you to have, you are no more use to them and they don't wish to speak to you. Try that for a hard thought. I can tell you it makes my lip make a moue as if I am sucking lemon.

Enough of these bitter thoughts, I have a wheatbag full; I am off to light the fire and pay some bills and write some letters and do some work. 'Redemption through work.' I sob as I hurl myself at the desk like a missile.

Tuesday, 13 May
Mary and George came back from the Blue Gum Forest late last night. They walked ten hours and were exhilarated, standing by the fire laughing as I stood in my dressing-gown pouring a sherry to warm them with a mild envy in my heart. In the

forest it was too dark to take photographs as the trees go straight up for a long, long way. Next time I will go too.

Everything is golden in the afternoon light and I am coughing and feeling useless. Today I went to town on the train and came back on the same day. It is better that way, I see now. It makes a trip less of a production, more casual and easily done.

In a park I ate lunch. Cheese and poppyseed bread I got from Cyril's delicatessen in Hay Street. A man who had been sleeping in the sun under an oak woke up and in his long curling hair oak leaves stuck like orchids. He looked so beautiful he could have been Miranda in *The Tempest*, but I think it wasn't a role the poor devil wanted, it was a drink.

Thursday, 15 May
Everything is changing. The trees are turning brown and the leaves are falling. Elizabeth has come to stay for part of her school holidays and points at the trees in pleasure. We sang all the way here on the train from town.

> *Essential oils are wrung*
> *The attar of the rose*
> *Is not expressed by suns alone*
> *It is the gift of screws.*

Mary gave me that quote when we were talking yesterday. No one can beat Emily Dickinson on suffering. She understood it as blood understands the vein.

Elizabeth, Mary and I have just come in from getting autumn leaves to dry and press. We walked down to Buttenshaw Bridge and up Lone Pine Road and home past Sarah's. We took plastic bags and under the flowering cherries in the streets, leaves lay splattered like a painter's palette as we cooed and bent and gathered showing specially good ones to each other before we dropped them in our bags.

If weather had a wardrobe, it's autumn dresses I like best. The tailoring of winter is very splendid and impressive, spring's chiffon and silks and then summer's cottons are undoubtedly seductive, but give me an autumn frock every time.

Friday, 16 May
All day Elizabeth and Mary have been dressing up in my old ball-gowns. We took photographs and now all the years of frustration over hopeless pictures and wasted money are redeemed. They are beautiful. Strapless gold taffeta over tan net frothing out below the skirt; or beaded net shining with black sequins over bare arms with a long drop of black crepe draped over the body ...

Sunday, 18 May
Early this morning I rode my bike over the trees' wealth of gold coinage. The paths that were pink with cherry blossom thick as icing are now gold and wet. Each month I love this place more.

George brought my bike back from the garage two days ago; two new tyres, and the chain fixed. Now watch me speed over these gold leaves.

Elizabeth has gone home; her father came to fetch her yesterday. We sat on Olympian Rock and watched a fog swirl round the Three Sisters and through the valley. The sun shone down on us with the fog creeping and wafting over us in the warmth as if we were in a humidi tent in a hospital ward, wheezing and coughing with our anxious mother outside watching and talking quietly. And speaking of coughing, the days here have my cough: a raucous rhythm to every hour. When Mary and I walked down to Buttenshaw Bridge all around the mountain tops shone in the sun with the bright blue sky above. Near the Three Sisters birds were calling and two white cockatoos screaming to each other their own surreal messages from some planet of madness where to sing is to scream, flew backwards and forwards above the gum-trees.

Friday, 23 May
Peri was on her hands and knees planting out seedlings called Angels' Wings when I told her my children's paternal grandmother had died. No one could get to her funeral in Adelaide and so late did we hear that not even flowers could be sent. I am in favour of sending flowers to the living and it needles me that I tried to send for some last week but my mother talked me out of

it. I stayed with Peri with the smooth blue sea outside the bedroom window and ferries sliding past between the Heads of the bay. In the big four-poster carved walnut bed I lay and felt wondrous sad. Mary, who is still here with me, but leaves to live in the city on Sunday said that she never goes to bed early when she is unhappy. She plays records, Gregorian chants, to get the full flavour of her suffering.

It is very cold today and the fire has three big logs at a time put on it. I have written letters and Mary has corrected a manuscript for me. I always thought I could spell quite nicely, but now I see I can't.

It is interesting to watch yourself in a period of grief. It seems to maintain itself at endurable levels, in my case at least. The truth is I am still sad, sad she says, I could howl like a chained dog at the moon, about leaving Mr Waterlily. It feels like cutting off one's own hand slowly in the night. Yet after an hour or so, the pain diminishes and I am now of the opinion that no pills or drink will help the healing hasten. Ah, but at times I have no sense of proportion, no courage and little hope. It will pass. I tell myself these three magical words over and over. Enough of this, the chimes are ringing in the wind, the fire is burning brightly, darkness is falling and two beautiful pink Pontiac potatoes are baking in their skins in the oven for our dinner. Don't you hate people who can eat in the midst of grief? Personally, I never really respected the person who ate a hearty breakfast while his wife lay dead in their bed. (I have seen it done.)

Saturday, 24 May
All night the chimes rang in the high wind. In the morning I found the wattle at the gate split with its yellow buds sprawled across the drive. Naturally I stood and sobbed. It seemed an omen. Dead tree. Dead affair.

I rode my bike home from Snaps with the wind going through my new emerald green scarf like a diamond cutter. The first ranunculi are up, two of them with dark green frills of leaves sprouting through the ash and oak-leaf mulch. Spring and hope here they come. In July, I have just heard, Blanche d'Alpuget,

Tim Winton and I are going to tour Tasmania to speak about writing. I have never been there nor have I met these two. Yes, I am excited.

Some days seem wrecked like ships. Some seem so close to the rocks they veer and sway and it is all I can do to keep my hand to the tiller, sweating and wide-eyed guiding this wild thing on to night.

Mary is leaving, Hugh is going to Duntroon and Granny's dead. Tonight an old friend of Mary's and who used to go to school dances with both of us in Adelaide when the girls were girls and men wore dinner suits, is coming to dinner. And please Lord don't let me sob into my roast dinner and disgrace myself.

> *The tyme away dothe waste*
> *And the tide, they say, tarrieth for no man.*
>
> (Nickolas Uvedale, *Ralph Roister Doister*, c. 1552)

I say this to pull myself together and stop the waste of weeping. To be a writer it is necessary to be particularly ruthless. Success does not lie day after day weeping and sobbing. Success gets up, dries its eyes and writes down something original and true, not waiting any longer for the tide to turn.

Monday, 26 May

I have been out planting roses. Isn't that a good sentence? I put in two climbing Peace roses. They are to grow up the steps and be big as teacups full of scent, pale yellow, frilled and frothy as egg nog. Grow rose grow. I put in two pink floribunda roses, hybrids, called Flamingo, and one bit of a white heaven called Misty plus another yellow one called Shasta.

Yesterday Sarah and I drove to Little Hartley over the mountain and down on to the plain that stretches then across Australia for thousands of kilometres. On the way back we stopped and saw the house we both tried to buy before we met each other, the advertisement for which brought us both to live in the mountains. A coincidence.

At Mount Boyce where the devil would freeze in spite of hell's own blasts, we stopped at a big nursery. I bought a Dove tree. Listen to this; it has white flowers like doves and is sometimes called a Handkerchief Tree because the flowers hang down like white linen handkerchiefs. Who could ever resist a tree like that. It is a stick at the moment, but so full of promises, promises. I got another clematis too, a pink rose coloured big one. Not sure yet where it will go.

After getting the plants, we lit a fire at the escarpment and grilled chops over gum leaves, ate a raddichio and avocado salad dressed with walnut oil, had bread, wine and the sun on our backs.

Mary has gone. I am alone, not lonely, considering this past year and what I might achieve in the next if anything. I think about the garden. Whatever losses and gains there are in one's life, at least the garden plugs on: the roots growing deeper, the branches wider, the trees taller, the bulbs multiply, the ground cover spreads, the roses grow bigger and even as I write, the white lilacs are budding. A body is like a garden. It has to be cared for, but without stern denials, such as weeding in the garden, it all runs to rot and ruin and is, in the end, not a working living thing at all, simply a wreck or a backyard or a dump. With these grim warnings I lash myself along to try to be braver than I was in this last week.

Thursday, 29 May
Phoney manure is better than no manure, so I rode up the street and bought some tree pellets. Now the citrus, growing fainter by the day, has been fed and the new roses have little bombs of food planted beside them. As I finished this, George arrived and stayed to lunch. We ate in the garden where the trees are naked and it looks so open and strange where once so recently all was red leafy and screened, curtained and easy. Now it is harsh and brave and bare.

Because, let's face it, I am in such trouble I can barely function. Everything takes longer and so few things get done. I feel as if I have been in a cage with a panther and not yet out of it, am so weary of the struggle to appear normal I can barely totter. All this to end a love affair.

Friday, 30 May
I wrote a poem called *Glass* this morning and ran out to the letter-box and posted it for the last day of a poetry contest. It seems reckless, but I won one once entering like that at the eleventh hour.

Today's blue sky could pierce your eye. It is a day for planting but I have nothing left to plant. Putting things in letter-boxes is a bit like planting.

I haven't spoken to anyone for twenty-four hours. This is a help for writing. Dusk is falling and a vague blush is growing up the horizon like a curtain, not dropping but growing to the sky.

~ 10 ~

June

One, two, pick up sticks. Three, four, open the door. Five, six ... oops, I have got it wrong. I have been out picking up sticks and I did lay them straight in my grate.

I went to town. There, at Hunters Hill, I had lunch with a friend on her verandah in the sun, eating smoked salmon and having a luscious gossip. She drove me around showing me the beautiful old houses of Hunters Hill and, among them, 'Passey', the home of Rachel Henning. Several of the houses are in a French style of architecture. It looks therefore a little bit like a collage of Sydney Harbour views, red coral trees and pointsettia, semi-tropical plants and, plomped down on this postcard, some eighteenth-century style French mansions. Makes you blink.

I went to Leichhardt and stayed with Mr Waterlily and there we healed our differences. What a two months it's been. Grief like that so affects the mind its like having a brain tumour. The simplest thing is an effort and it makes words get spelt partly backwards.

And now, before I got out to plant the Dove tree, listen to this from Macoby's *What Tree is That?* 'The Dove Tree. Family: *Davidiceae.* Just over seventy years ago, this beautiful tree caused a botanical sensation when it flowered for the first time in the West in the garden of a French collector named de Vilmorin. This came as the climax of a race between French and English botanists to find and flower a tree reported from Western China by the French missionary Père David. It had ghostly white flowers fluttering among the foliage like handkerchiefs, or so he reported ...' Now here I go to plant this miracle and may Heaven bless this tree and all who see it flower. Peace at last.

Well, the deed is done, as Macbeth may have said to his lady. And so straight and tall it is, near the two young dogwoods I planted last year.

How I long for a bag of bulbs. I want to throw them on to the lawn. Then plant them where they fall. This gives the easy natural look I long for. Edna Walling used to throw down potatoes, Lydia said, and where they fell she would plant birches. Yes, and I'd like a couple of dozen birches down my lane while we're at it too, thanks. And how I'd love to hire ten men for ten days. It's like a school arithmetic puzzle. 'How much would it cost to hire ten men for ten days at a hundred dollars at day?' The answer, I think, is a thousand dollars.

I'd have a proper trellis put up for the clematis at the back steps, a pergola with wisteria and jasmine to climb over it, an arch over the gate with clematis and roses to climb through that, a set of wide low steps down the lane made from railway sleepers and there the avenue of birches, and at the end of the avenue a bench to sit on reading or dreaming. And in the street I want to plant five flowering cherries. And at the gate David suggests a liquid amber. They grow so vast but even young are brilliant and to see them now, down the Mall in Leura, is enough to send anyone straight off to the nursery.

Now to make some Yunang tea. I got several packets of tea today with a cheque I had from poems. A weight is sitting in my brain like one of those old black two-pound lumps of lead my mother used to weigh out fruit for jam. It's from the grief I think, even though now it's over. Or is it a giant's black boot pressing down its weight? Or is it merely that I need a nap.

I caught a rat in a trap. It is planted now under a rose called Tiffany. I plan to turn that rat into a pink rose.

News at last from Woolfie and Gordon. Now I can send letters as they have a whitewashed mud and brick house in the Peleponnese.

Thursday, 5 June
How the ivy grows. And the jasmine and the honeysuckle. And the cotoneaster. That worst of all. If I could dig it out I would. My arms are too weak or something, they simply turn to jelly and the thing sits there and gloats. I have been out, though, cutting all this back with a feeling of vengeance in my heart. I've noticed tasks bring their own emotions. For instance, knitting or

embroidering are calming things. Digging is a little bit aggressive but feels healthy. Cutting back tough things makes me feel malicious. Weeding makes me feel tough and, later, virtuous. Planting makes me happy. Oh yes, it does. I would plant all day if I had things to plant.

Andrew and Mary are coming up for the weekend. The fire is roaring and I have been thinking about gardening. The fact is, I don't think I am making a very good job of this garden. I have so much to learn and there is so much to do. For example, someone told me it is not a good idea to put all the ash on the azaleas as I had done, as it is alkaline and they are acid-loving plants.

Gardening seems to need so much self-discipline, restraint, taste, energy, optimism, imagination and just plain strength. All things I am feeling rather low on at the moment; and things no bank can lend me either. I often think of David and Lydia taking out the magnolia because it was in the wrong place. That must have felt like killing a peacock in paradise. A kind of ruthless vision. Not at all sentimental; that won't do for a gardener.

Friday, 6 June

Every day that I do nothing in the garden I think of the ivy and the weeds winning and the chaos of nature slowly creeping over all my ardent and best efforts. I want, I want, I want, oh, I want a beautiful garden.

The clematis I planted last week by the front verandah is wilting, in a crisis and I stand there like a physician quietly wringing my hands. Staring at it, half-defeated by the mystery with only a dripping hose as a medicine for its crisis. The equivalent, I suppose, of sips of lemonade hourly for someone needing, if the truth be known, a large and hasty blood transfusion.

Today is the first time in weeks my mind has worked without feeling as if it needed an oil change. What angel sat all day on my shoulder, smiling and fanning my face with a feather? It's a miracle of relief. And now, by the fire, after a hot bath, drinking Earl Grey tea, I say there is not much wrong with my world. These mountains, these holy, holy mountains. When I came to live in the mountains I was determined to be happy. And today I think I might have a very good chance.

It was in an atmosphere like this with the fire crackling and outside the cold gathering like arms around the house, that Coleridge wrote one of my favourite poems in all the world. A great, great poem. It's called *Frost at Midnight*.

Saturday, 7 June
There's a big road map of Greece spread out on the table and Andrew and I are searching the Peleponnese for Gortynias where Woofie and Gordon are living. No luck.

We walked down to the wild white gums, now shedding their bark and growing more silver by the day. Like an elegant woman, silver streaking down like age's graceful paint. We grilled lamb chops on a fire, looked up at the blue sky, drank the wine, and made each other laugh.

Mary arrived after lunch and then we went off to George's party where a band played Porgy and Bess. Some danced, I stood and watched and felt very, very old. It was a twenty-first birthday party for a girl called Hilary and there is nothing like being with the age-group of one's children *en masse* to make you feel foolish as an old sock. I watched Hilary sit on the steps outside and light the candles on her cake (so no one could see). As Andrew said: 'This is a post-modern party Kate.' In other words, do not expect any of the traditions to be kept, except in the quirkiest referential way. The white carnations and white camellias I had put around the candles gleamed and with one puff it was over. Her loving father, camera hanging from his neck, took a flashlight or two and now posterity will have a flat piece of paper of an event so multi-dimensional and packed with feeling, memory and hope.

Monday, 9 June
Elizabeth came here for her twelfth birthday party yesterday. We had a picnic in a wind cutting like a saw through bone. Here at home her friends sat around this table with her father, Mary and myself, and blew out the candles.

Today George and Mary and I sat in the sun by the cliffs with a fire blazing and had yet another picnic. I have this absolute passion for them, especially now because each day reminds me

Frost at Midnight

The Frost performs its secret ministry,
Unhelped by any wind. The owlet's cry
Came loud – and hark, again! loud as before.
The inmates of my cottage, all at rest,
Have left me to that solitude, which suits
Abstruser musings: save that at my side
My cradled infant slumbers peacefully.
'Tis calm indeed! so calm, that it disturbs
And vexes meditation with its strange
And extreme silentness. Sea, hill, and wood,
This populous village! Sea, and hill, and wood,
With all the numberless goings-on of life,
Inaudible as dreams! the thin blue flame
Lies on my low-burnt fire, and quivers not;
Only that film, which fluttered on the grate,
Still flutters there, the sole unquiet thing.
Methinks, its motion in this hush of nature
Gives it dim sympathies with me who live,
Making it a companionable form,
Whose puny flaps and freaks the idling Spirit
By its own moods interprets, every where
Echo or mirror seeking of itself,
And makes a toy of Thought.

But O! how oft,
How oft, at school, with most believing mind,
Presageful, have I gazed upon the bars,
To watch that fluttering *stranger*! and as oft
With unclosed lids, already had I dreamt
Of my sweet birth-place, and the old church-tower,
Whose bells, the poor man's only music, rang
From morn to evening, all the hot Fair-day,
So sweetly, that they stirred and haunted me
With a wild pleasure, falling on mine ear
Most like articulate sounds of things to come!
So gazed I, till the soothing things, I dreamt,
Lulled me to sleep, and sleep prolonged my dreams!
And so I brooded all the following morn,
Awed by the stern preceptor's face, mine eye

Fixed with mock study on my swimming book;
Save if the door half opened, and I snatched
A hasty glance, and still my heart leaped up,
For still I hoped to see the *stranger*'s face,
Townsman, or aunt, or sister more beloved,
My play-mate when we both were clothed alike!

Dear babe, that sleepest cradled by my side,
Those gentle breathings, heard in this deep calm,
Fill up the interspersèd vacancies
And momentary pauses of the thought!
My babe so beautiful! it thrills my heart
With tender gladness thus to look at thee,
And think that thou shalt learn far other lore,
And in far other scenes! For I was reared
In the great city, pent 'mid cloisters dim,
And saw nought lovely but the sky and stars.
But *thou*, my babe! shalt wander like a breeze
By lakes and shady shores, beneath the crags
Of ancient mountain, and beneath the clouds,
Which image in their bulk both lakes and shores
And mountain crags: so shalt thou see and hear
The lovely shapes and sounds intelligible
Of that eternal language which thy God
Utters, who from eternity doth teach
Himself in all, and all things in himself.
Great universal Teacher! he shall mould
Thy spirit, and by giving make it ask.

Therefore all seasons shall be sweet to thee,
Whether the summer clothe the general earth
With greenness, or the redbreast sit and sing
Betwixt the tufts of snow on the bare branch
Of mossy apple-tree, while the nigh thatch
Smokes in the sun-thaw; whether the eave-drops fall
Heard only in the trances of the blast,
Or if the secret ministry of frost
Shall hang them up in silent icicles,
Quietly shining to the quiet moon.

SAMUEL TAYLOR COLERIDGE

it will soon be too late. Once winter slams down the Mall, we will all be fog- or snow-bound.

George has hurt his back so afterwards, home here, he lay by the fire while I rubbed him with Dencorub until he almost feel asleep. The constant pain makes his face look as if it will creak. Now everyone has gone home and I am alone by the fire and not ungrateful either.

Saturday, 14 June

All week I have been in the city. I wrote some poems, saw a film, had lunch with Hugh, went to a party with Caroline, and stayed with Mary. I went to the Biennale of Sydney with Ian, my old friend from Adelaide. Two sculptures sit in my mind like old men. One was a white room with yellow pollen on the shiny painted white floor and a spotlight overhead on that pure glowing square of pollen like a thousand flowers' crushed haloes. It was quiet, glowing, pure and strange.

The other was a performance written about on a wall with a small film of it on television nearby. Joseph Beuys spent several weeks dressed in felt with a walking stick in a room with a coyote. It sounds cruel (for the animal, that is) but it didn't seem so.

Sunday, 15 June

Down in the valley a lyrebird called to a lyrebird. Sitting on Olympian Lookout with Mr Waterlily we heard the magical song float over the trees. Down in the valley, a lyrebird calling out his passion. The music Malcolm Williamson composed for the ballet *The Display* was there, floating up like the sea. We sat and stared over the blue space and every now and then looked at each other and smiled and said: 'Yes, it is. It really is.'

There is a light mist swirling round the trees and on the lawn seven red-and-blue rosellas picked at some seed or insect they had found.

There is a poem I learned at school that floats through my mind when I see parrots. Where it came from or how it ends I do not know. This is it:

Some where some when
I've seen
But where or when I cannot tell
Three parrots flying
Out of shrill green...

Apart from hymns and songs, that is the only poem I remember from my schooling.

And now to lay myself down by this sweet fire and have a sleep. And so I did.

Two Red Cross women have been to call. They are selling Afghan rugs that I would like to buy. The sleep so fast induced lying under one of these rugs is an innocent one. It has to be felt to be understood. I don't know why it is. Perhaps the weight of the wool mixed as it is with air because of the wide holes in the crochet pattern, the fact hands sat toiling over it and made it human, soft and female; I don't know. Whatever it is, it works like a drug. I go down like a felled tree.

Monday, 16 June
Three red leaves in the white fog outside the white curtains in my bedroom.

The water from the tap is so cold it could break your teeth off. I have been outside pulling up ivy around the big daphne which is inscrutably dying. Mr Waterlily stood beside it two days ago and told me so. I rushed to turn the hose on but he scratched the crowded ground around it and told me it was damp. The ivy is fierce like wire. My hands feel as if they have been building fences. The ivy had the daphne by the throat. If I could I'd call a policeman and have the ivy arrested.

As I walked on the path in the bush after hearing the lyrebird sing I thought again how sexy the bush is. Everything is ardently multiplying by courting and copulating and killing and dying too. It is busier than a main street. I think a lot about that lyrebird. I would like to write an ode to it. Was it the same thing in Keats, that hearing that nightingale song touched his heart as if it were an instrument? Are we all in the end to play in unison?

Today, it feels as if winter has arrived. Scarves and hats and gloves and fog and icy water.

Wednesday, 18 June

I have a new woodbox. It is rough, rugged and beautiful, made of thick sticks woven in a circle. I saw it in a shop, walked home and found in the mail some poems paid for. I rode back and carried it home on the back of the bike like a demented heroic ant. Now here it is, full of logs beside the fire. It looks as if it has been knitted by a giant.

I came home from town this morning and as I got off the train, winter's stalactite licked me like a tongue as I ran down the Mall all the way home. In front of me the mountains glowed blue as sapphires in the clear, cold bright light. I love this place.

And, as for my trip to town, all night we dragged the bottom of the ocean for silver and gold fish. In the morning I came home feeling like a silk doll who caught the Emperor's favourite fish, the gold and sacred one.

Thursday, 19 June

Two red leaves left. Yes, a sentence as reduced as the thing it describes. I lie in bed and watch these two red flags left from autumn's battle, valiant but doomed. Winter's won. It's all over but the leaving.

As I lay in the bath this morning I watched in the top of a tall gum against the skyline and a white cockatoo shining like a knife in the wind.

Friday, 20 June

I feel as if I have narrowly escaped prison and am puffing with relief. The post brought my tax assessment for the past five years. Each year on a separate form added by Sarah when I ran round to her asking her to decipher it, a vast sum. I sat in her armchair staring and wondering if I could be made to sell my house. Then I thought of prison because Sarah said some people are sent to goal for overdue taxes. I knew prison would give me a nervous breakdown; just thinking of loss of freedom and bars over windows makes me break out in a sweat. I stumbled home and rang the tax accountant who had filled out the form. I was told it was only the first page, not the addition of all, and that I would not have to sell my house nor go to prison. With $3,300 now to pay, I wept for relief. That amount seems a mere bagatelle but where it will come from I can't tell. A lottery? I have eighty cents to last until some magazine pays for a poem sometime. I could write a cheque at the Village Store for food, but I think it might bounce. These days test character I tell myself sternly as, shaking, I step into a hot bath. I like the freedom of not being married but I don't like the responsibility.

Saturday, 21 June
One red leaf swinging in the cold bright wind like a hanging man.

There was a frost last night. The cineraria's leaves are like white plates but do not seemed to have burned. (The label said they were prone to frost.)

I have been out planting slips of white carnations left over from the flowers Mr Waterlily sent. I absent-mindedly stuck one in last week and I see now it has taken. So I got the rest from the compost.

My poem *The Story* which I wrote here is in the *Sydney Morning Herald* today. I see I have become much more aware of the sky since I have been here and it has affected my writing.

Sunday, 22 June
Winter solstice. The shortest day of the year and this has been our first real week of winter. My toes are cold, but the tea is hot. It is soup weather. Yesterday at Snaps David was wearing his woollen cap for the first time this year.

Last night the full moon over the pine-trees gleamed like a gold sovereign and rose higher as if flung up by a careless buccaneer, jubilant to have found so much in the coffers of the ship he had just so heartlessly scuttled.

As I rode down the main street this morning in my quilted silk and down coat, the liquid amber trees were glowing like a row of glasses of claret waiting for the men to come out from the

~151~

boardroom for a hasty lunch. They are even cut in the shape of glasses to allow the electricity wires to pass through their ruined centres. On the way home I saw a flock of bower birds fly up from a garden. I didn't see the male, but there were over a dozen females or young there. That means at least they are still about, even if the currawongs I have fed have chased them from my garden. How to get them back, that's the trick.

Have you ever lain down by a wood fire to read and fallen asleep? To wake up after that sleep is a little bit like waking up as a child with your mother smiling at you.

Yesterday I took my wheelbarrow down to the escarpment and got a load of kindling. This morning I had coffee with Sarah and she gave me some bright red woollen socks, some pale green long johns and a red-and-blue tartan mohair shawl. It is her belief I am not wearing enough clothing and I think perhaps she is quite right.

Monday, 23 June
Eight daffodils are through. Poking like the sharp beaks of chickens through the earth's hard shell. Now with winter solstice passed and these green arrows, spring is coming.

I walked to Katoomba wrapped in layers like an arctic explorer and going past some berry bushes, saw a flock of bower birds feeding. I stood quietly thinking that with so many females surely there must be a male nearby and suddenly there, hopping in his typical way, was that small dark blue king. My blue angel. I always feel somehow grace has fallen or a blessing been given when I see that blue male. A drop of blue ink flung in the eye.

The cinerarias are black from frost. They look poisoned and in a way I suppose they are. So now I know not to plant cinerarias again.

Thursday, 26 June
I have been to town to the dentist among other things. I rush to the mirror from time to time and bare my teeth with pleasure. Snarling happily at myself. As for the cost, I'll think of that later. Along with all those other notes piling up saying people

or, rather, firms, are getting less and less friendly to me by the week.

I saw George's old multi-coloured station wagon when I got out from the train in wind like diamond cutters. I found him eating soup in the Pumpkin Inn. I went in and ordered some potato and spinach soup for myself. He drove me home and while he lit the wood fire, I lit the gas fire and turned on the radiator and boiled the kettle. Then, like an old married couple, we settled down; he to read the paper, I to open my mail and both to drinking coffee.

Perhaps this is how easy a good marriage could be. Rhythm in work like the rocking of a boat. I made more of the same soup we'd had for lunch. I see now I have had almost an entire bunch of spinach since I have come home. Will I have green hair?

I stayed at Leichhardt with Mr Waterlily and spent the night sleeping as saints joined like scissor blades.

Friday, 27 June
A good day. I rolled up the hose and hung it on a tap. Suddenly the front garden looked neat. More ivy pulled out and hacked back. I have found if you eat enough you don't feel so cold. Having the wood fire going from early morning is a help. The Aboriginal people have had a saying in some places that, depending on the degree of cold, it is either a three-dog night or a four-dog night. Well, here it is three logs at a time that need to go on, so it is a three-log day today.

Andrew Grafton is coming to stay. I have been running out to see if he is coming up the Mall, but so far, not yet.

I have been making brownies. I always read about them in American books and felt irritated that there was no description. Now I know what they are: chocolate squares with soft centres.

By the way, the policeman who came to live in my house went off and got married.

Monday, 30 June
Census Day tomorrow and I'll be in prison. I told my Mother on the telephone this morning that for two days I was to teach in an ex-prison at Lithgow. She said she hoped I wouldn't have

things thrown at me. I said, 'Ex-prison, Mother'. It is for High School students and is an arts camp. How I dread it. At night I am to have a cell with a bed in it and nothing else. George lent me his sleeping-bag and I put it in a plastic rubbish bag and rode with it to the newsagent so I can collect it in the morning when I get the early train.

Yesterday Sarah, Andrew, George and I took some food and went down to the escarpment and once again, with my usual relish, I lit a small fire. More and more bark until it flared high and then I was happy. And I was laughing with them all afternoon until we came home, put our feet in socks near the fire here, drank coffee and they all left. I fell asleep by the fire and that is one of the best ways to pass a day I know.

Today the sun was out and I felt a wild determination to do it all again. No one to share a picnic with and I was planning to go alone to light the fire when I met Craig End and he came with me with his small dog Molly. We grilled chicken, lamb kidneys and lamb chops and had that with fennel and olive salad.

I walked round the Denisons' garden this morning. It is bare and romantic with just, as David says, the scaffolding of the trees bared. The Himalyan pear tree is covered with buds and reaches high to the blue sky. That tree is one of my favourites in this world. It is engaged to Spring and waiting to appear as a bride.

~ 11 ~

July

Wednesday, 2 July

Home after the camp. I loved it. I slept in a cell in my clothes, with no heating and no light with children yelling and banging on doors until two a.m. I ate the worst food I have had in my life, hamburgers without buns, dried packet soup, white bread, tea from great urns with powdered milk, and so on and all of it was delicious and I ate more heartily than I have in months. I have been off my tucker. Put an orchid in a farmyard garden and if it was sickly, it may well flourish.

Last night in the cold with my nose tucked into my mohair tartan scarf I walked home down the Mall and felt happy, grateful and very proud. I reckon I am a good teacher, even if I haven't been trained. I have a theory that I use – that my native cunning, desperation and luck combined to get me through.

My theory is that, since it is said the brain is very like a computer, if all the entrances which take messages to the computer are used, it is more likely that the message will get through to the machine. So, I use everything from sound to give colour to their tongues and set mine working too. I play tapes of poets reading their work, I read to them, they read, we walk and talk and look, they write, I write; I aim for a continual state of intense excitement. Afterwards I am half-dead and, hopefully, they have learnt something about their abilities and they have learnt to feel some quiver of passion, if they didn't before, about poetry.

Sunday, 6 July

The Penguin Book of Australian Women Poets now exists. Clare O'Brien rang from Penguin in Melbourne on Wednesday and said: 'Congratulations, it's a girl!' Next day I went to town and had lunch with Andrew and Mary at E.J.'s to celebrate. Jean took me to see *The Seagull* at the Opera House that night. Chekov, if I had to choose from all my favourite writers, is the one I like the best. I had lunch with Caroline next day at Café Troppo on Glebe Point Road. There I had George Papaellinas pointed out to me who is coming to Tasmania on the tour this week. Last week I pruned the roses. I had no real understanding of the shape needed, so I cut where I thought. I wish, I wish, I wish I could plant some more. I long for hundreds. A woman can't have too many roses, in my opinion.

More daffodils are putting up their green thumbs through the earth like hitchhikers. They want the clouds to stop.

Yesterday Mr Waterlily came here and we took a picnic down to Lyrebird Dell. We lit a fire under the overhanging rock and sat drinking claret waiting for the chops to cook, not at all unhappy. What will happen to us, heaven knows. If I were a betting woman, I would not put money on us. Yet he stands there beside the waterfall, and I do not know where to put my love. I want to run away. No matchmaker worth her salt would put us together. We are so unsuited yet all I want is to hold his hand in the night, turn, sigh and be happy lying there like children.

Who can chart the heart's path? It has its own rules and tells no one what they are. Keeping its own counsel, it makes its choice, closes its mouth and will never tell how or why that choice was made.

I rode fast down the street this morning, the trees shining in the sun and the wind cold, very, very cold. My bicycle lapped the road like a tongue and I felt happy and sensuous tearing through the air like a flame.

I am packing to go to Tasmania. You can come too, if you like. I have seen the itinerary. Every day a different town and we three writers do a performance there, then pack and go. I am not afraid, simply excited, overwrought, like a baroque balcony.

Wednesday, 9 July
Tasmania at last! As the captain said to the convict after an anxious voyage.

I am in Burnie. We drove to the airport and met George Papaellinas and soon, after dinner, we are off to give our first performance. And may heaven bless this enterprise, I say. I am having a brandy for courage. Oh, wish me luck. I am trying to eschew the feeling that I hold the whole weight of women's writing on my shoulders. That is rot, I know it, but it is a thought I have. God, it's cold.

Friday, 11 July
Tasmania reminds me of Scotland. Launceston, where we are today, is very like a Highland town. I walked down a hill with George from the ABC studios with a valley falling away on one side and around us black-and-white houses, elegant, neatly preserved and smart as only black and white can be. There is no colour rioting here; things are restrained. One feels people know their place and keep to it. A feeling here of a harsh past. A rigid character, restrained, but not unattractive. Things are formal. I would not walk laughing down the street here in a long velvet skirt. No sir.

We do up to three performances a day and go from town to town like well-paid gypsies. I should have big gold earrings. My head hurts. I feel as if I have been scalped. I want some brown bread and my own bed. Though I am kindly treated, I am short-tempered.

Sunday, 13 July
Hobart has a hill with snow. As I walked out this morning I looked up and there it was, strange as a peacock flying over. What a shock.

George does not care for nature. When I stop to look at a plant he almost shudders. I told him the names of some flowers and shrubs. Then I saw a full-blown rose, yellow tinged with peach. I asked him if he knew the name. He said: 'That's a camellia, isn't it?' This, I think, is quite rare. A rose may smell by any other name, but a camellia does not.

The town is utterly unlike any other Australian city. It is solid, reeking like a fire with history. I can almost hear the convicts' chains clanging as they sadly and miserably shuffle down the street to work. Yesterday Michael Denholm, our host, and I saw a ball and chain and ankle clamp in a window of an antique shop. Swallow that fact like an iron ball, if you can, as the Zen master might say.

The houses and many of the public buildings here sit neat as stamps on their piece of land as if it were an envelope. They seem stuck on. By this I mean there are few verandahs and the plain square of the building with its grey slate roof seems surprisingly without props to the mainlander's eye. It is stone and stone and stone built round a harbour.

Tuesday, 15 July
I have been to the mountain with Tim and Denise Winton and their two-year-old son Jesse. We threw snowballs and went a bit mad with Jesse sliding down small slopes probably thinking that it was ice-cream. This is a dazzling place. The water bleeding blue among the hills goes on and sweeps from left to right and no one could know walking these proper streets what wilderness, wild weather, snow and grand things lie behind. Like having a mad and passionate aunt, severely collared in lace with a whaleboned waist, a long black taffeta skirt, who, at night goes mad, dances naked on the white frosted lawn and sings songs to Aboriginal gods with her hair flying and her heart pounding with wild unrequited love. In the morning, she comes in, brushes her hair, neatly coils it in a bun, pins it tightly, puts on her skirt and black leather shoes and, bending her head oh so modestly, mildly pours the tea at breakfast.

Wednesday, 16 July
Yesterday at the Botanical Gardens with Sarah Day; all in black she strode around like a young thin brave witch among her plants. By the pond we watched the ducks with dark green velvet heads gliding round. Then Sarah strode off in her flat shiny black patent laceup shoes to a hothouse. Plants with leaves like painted plates sat in the hot wet air. It is a good place for lust. I found a gardener who told me about leather-wood trees.
   Tomorrow George and I fly back to Sydney.

Saturday, 19 July
Frost at Leura. As I walked out this morning the ground was white and all the cinerarias have given up the ghost. They

mouldered away while I was gone. No tulips yet but plenty of daffodils. Soon, too, the hyacinths are due. Behind me a curra-wong flew like a stealthy Indian in a forest. Watching. What it didn't know, was I was hearing. There is not a cloud in the sky, the cold wind that yesterday sliced me like a magician's lady has gone. I can feel a picnic coming on. If I can only find someone to come with me.

I looked at this poor scrap of a garden this morning, and wondered why I had toiled so long for so little. This perhaps is simply what every gardener feels in winter, but I think not entirely. Weeds are coming on in waves like a Persian army. Here I stand feeling like Athens, nervous but determined. I really need a hand with this. If only I could get old Waterlily up here. He is good at weeding. Knows what's what.

George and I flew out of Hobart on Wednesday and glad we were too in the face of threatened pilot strikes and petrol shortages. He makes me laugh so much he only has to raise his shoulders a little and I begin to smile. At Colville Cottage in Hobart we said goodbye to Tim and Denise and Jesse. And so soon the group was broken. Just as fast as it had formed and bonded, then we parted. But these people will be my friends. And coming from me that is a promise not lightly dashed on rocks.

Caroline has been staying here while I was away. I can feel her presence. Even to be where she has been makes me happy. Why am I so happy? The answer is, I think, because I'm home. Now I'm off to paint my lips blood-red and ride my bike to Snaps, taking under my arm like a seagull with her lunch box, the Penguin book.

Sunday, 20 July
An almost full moon is hanging like a baroque pearl round the sky's throat on a chain of stars.

Monday, 21 July
Today I walked to Katoomba to pay my electricity bill before it was cut off. The Cootamundra wattle is out. Small bright yellow, baby cotton balls on the dark green branches wave round every corner. Parrots fly over and no one is about.

Sitting up in bed at six p.m., my wet hair in a towel, my nose in a book, Mr Waterlily rang to say tonight he'll bring up my luggage left at Leichhardt after the trip to Tasmania. The leap would make a kangaroo envious. The bath is cleaned, the sheets changed to double, dishes done, papers pushed under the bed, I am calm and smiling and look ... this is how I live all the time.

Thursday, 24 July

I went to town early next morning after that visit. We drove down the mountain with the moon like a silver fruit. I could have plucked it especially for him. The dawn rose up like a baby's blanket being slowly pushed back in sleep. Horses grazed in the mist on the plain searching for some truth that horses long to know from their history. The mist shrouded it.

I stayed in bed at Leichhardt with a cold organising on the telephone the party and reading for the release of the new book.

I wrote some poems too.

It is difficult for writers not to feel guilty unless they are visibly hard at work hour after hour, day after day. I feel guilty when I see others go hastily off to their work. When Arthur Miller was married to Marilyn Monroe he said that his wife found it hard to understand that when he was looking out the window, he was working. I am not saying others give me hard looks, in fact I am kindly treated, but I feel the apparent idleness is like an insult to them at times.

Friday, 25 July

There's snow in my hair. It looks like small white flowers and I'm smiling. Nobody else here to see it. Who can I ring to tell? No one, they are all at work. I have no wood left and have rung the woodman. The gas is working hard.

Today the first hyacinth showed itself. Like a hand with all the leaves together pointing upwards as if waiting for a flower to be placed just there between them where later it will bloom.

Sunday, 27 July

It snowed for hours and the world turned white as if it had played in flour. Next day when I woke it was all still there.

After a while it began to look normal. How quickly we adjust.

I am trying to avoid saying something that I think I must. Philippa, who comes to Snaps and talks to me about gardening, has lost her son. Alexis was twenty-two and he jumped out of a window on Thursday night.

Yesterday David, Lydia and I went to her house to get it ready for her homecoming. She had been with him in town when it happened. We walked back to Snaps through the snow after we'd lit the fire and mopped up the burst pipe that was flooding the bathroom. I do not know what to say. Alexis' funeral is here at St Albyns church on Wednesday.

Monday, 28 July

The snow has gone. There were patches left in the shady spots in the garden, but today all's melted. The bower birds are back. On Saturday Mr Waterlily and I sat in the sunroom and watched these fat green birds hop around the lawn. I strained to watch and wait for the blue male to come. But he didn't. Only the hollyhocks and the pansies of the annuals I planted have survived the frost and snow. I think it's more than a nuisance that a local florist sells plants that cannot live here.

I am trying to write to Hugh every day. He is camping, the man on the phone said, when I rang Duntroon. It is snowing in Canberra. I think about him a lot and how I resent the satires of anxious mothers. The army has taken him in a gulp and only silence remains.

I think I will walk to Katoomba and see if the bank will let me have some money. I love the walk through the bush with Leura Cascades falling down over the rocks with the ferns and gum trees hanging over. Some day I expect to meet a fox or a lyrebird. I travel hopefully with my basket on my arm and my scarf around my throat.

George arrived with eight empty flagons to get water because his pipes have burst. I had no water for several hours on Friday. Glad I was to have had a jug of water on the table to make tea. I had the most miserable wash with the water from the hot-water bottle and had just finished when the pipes began to gurgle.

~ 12 ~

August

Saturday, 2 August

D has come to stay. I am glad to have her here because I am so sad. I went to Alexis' funeral with Craig last Wednesday. Afterwards Philippa invited us all back to Snaps where we drank champagne and talked in an atmosphere unlike any I have ever known. A sort of tragic jubilation. A grieving celebration of life. I felt quite mad and could not understand what people said to me. I walked home down the Mall wishing only to get terribly drunk. Because I keep no alcohol here in the house, I took a bath and went to bed and wished I was not alone nor that boy alone out there nor his mother to endure what must now be endured.

I have planted a white camellia beside the front window. D and I walked back from Snaps in the freezing wind planning to collect kindling from the escarpment and to do some replanting.

I went to town the day after the funeral as I was too sad to stay here alone. I swore, as I suppose most people do, that I will be better to others and not say cruel things and will part sweetly and lovingly every time from those I love. I think we are all living here or there, in this case on top of a mountain, inside a sort of eggshell of a reality we have invented, not really very much in touch with the facts. Perhaps it is the only way we can live. Things seem so important until you see that open grave, Mother Earth waiting as if in reverse childbirth to take back her own. Even more now, art seems less questionable than ever. If we have no art what are we?

I have just been watering the garden; I think it is a drought. No tulips up as yet, but more hyacinths have come. Two foxgloves are getting ready to bloom. I want five hundred. Well, one hundred then.

Today I got onto a source of horse manure. As I sat at Snaps next to June who hadn't been before, I remembered she rode horses. She says she has loads and loads of manure and that I can come and get some anytime. I met George soon afterwards and said I had found a source and could we go in his car tomorrow. Yes. Hooray.

Tonight I am cooking a chicken on the open fire in the dining-room with Dijon mustard covering it, and my griller holding it. I expect a great mess but it may be delicious. At least it makes a change from the vegetable soup I make day after day. I am grumpy and cooked out. There is nothing I really wish to eat or cook. This will pass no doubt but it takes a lot of fun out of life. My Mother, who was a dressmaker, got sewn out. So did Coco Chanel. They both said so. If people have to work so hard there is no time to balance the work with other things, the creativity dries up and there is just no more. You ask them what they have made recently and with a vague look they say casually, as if talking of a stranger's life work, 'Oh, I don't do that anymore'.

Sunday, 3 August

A sunny day. Leura with its air at its neck-snapping best. The trees stretched to the sky etching their description of winter. I have just been for a walk with D and later we are having a barbecue. Naturally. Speaking of that, the chicken over the open fire was a success. I recommend it to you. Dijon mustard slathered over it first helps and lemon juice, if you have it, is good. Then, just a twist or two of pepper and hop to it.

Here's something Melville write in *Moby Dick*:

> But Faith, like a jackal, feeds among the tombs, and even from these dead doubts she gathers here most vital hope.
>
> It needs scarcely to be told, with what feelings on the eve of a Nantucket voyage, I regarded these marble tablets, and by the murky light of that darkened, doleful day read the fate of the whalemen who had gone before me. Yes, Ishmael, the same fate may be thine....
>
> 'Yes, there is death in this business of whaling – a speechlessly quick chaotic bundling of a man into Eternity. But what then? Methinks we have hugely mistaken this matter of Life and Death. Methinks that what they call my shadow here on earth is my true substance. Methinks that in looking at things spiritual, we are too much like oysters observing the sun through water, and thinking that thick

~ 163 ~

water the thinnest of air. Methinks my body is but the lees of my better being. In fact take my body who will, take it I say, it is not me. And therefore three cheers for Nantucket; and come a stove boat and stove body when they will, for stove my soul, Jove himself cannot.

D and I have been out with the wheelbarrow gathering wood. I have also cut back with a lot of revengeful vigour the ivy on the side of the house where the fence is falling down.

Monday, 4 August
Not only morning has broken; so has the drought. It has rained almost all night and it still is. Just the day George and I are donning our rubber boots to go off to the horse stables to get what I so ardently long for. I invited Philippa because she is keen on gardens too, but she isn't quite up to it so is coming to lunch instead. I am making cardamom cake and a queer vegetable and rice casserole with a mustard sauce. It may be terrible or it may not.

Tuesday, 5 August
God help me through the next three days. Tonight our poetry book is being introduced at the Harold Park Hotel in Glebe. In the next two days, beginning at seven-thirty a.m. when I get collected to do a live television national interview, I have twenty interviews. Tears come to my eyes when I think of it. I suppose the truth is I am simply afraid I might not be able to do it well. I simply mustn't drink tonight, but I expect I will.

It has rained hour after hour. A strong wind has blown the chimes all night. They seem so friendly and consoling to me. Like a grandfather clock.

Yesterday George and I couldn't go to get the manure as it was raining too hard. Philippa talked over lunch about Alexis.

Well, in the rain, here I go. With trepidation and sweating. I hope, I hope, I hope ...

Saturday, 9 August
Floods. Big floods. Drums. Big drums. They beat for three nights and days. People died. Much was swept away. As you see, I'm still here.

I came home yesterday. The big wattle in full bloom is down. Is it an omen? Sarah can't live in her house. The row of pine trees across the road at Leuralla were damaged. They are the ones so tall they look like busbies in the sky. One fell across the road on to a shed and another is leaning ominously.

I have just ridden round to Sarah's. It looks like war. The tree like a fallen Goliath lies mutilated and beaten. Smaller trees were broken in its fall. Everywhere debris and great logs as men cut it up.

A worse sight is down at Gordon Falls lookout where one of the truly great trees of the mountains has fallen. A huge white snow gum. Like a fallen elephant as I said to a man working taking away logs. He said: 'Funny you should say that. I was thinking how like a dead whale it is.' He had been involved with a whale rescue on the North Coast and the worst part, he said, was burying the dead ones. I really loved that tree. The council worker said it is estimated now that the winds got to two hundred kilometres an hour.

In the city I did twenty interviews in two days and only blew one.

Sunday, 10 August
A calm clear day. The weather is smiling benevolently saying, 'What? Who? Me?' in the most innocent fashion. Any judge would be impressed. But all around lies the evidence – mayhem. I have been around to Sarah's with a man of the trees, in a manner of speaking. He is to give a report to a lawyer on his opinion of the safety of the pines. My thin teenage art nouveau gum is split. But something may save it. Prayer maybe. What would I do in the bath without it to shield the naked moon? Wash my toes and think of other things, I suppose. Something by Albinoni is being played on the radio and outside the sparrows are twittering, happy as I am for this calm day.

Chicken soup with fresh herbs from my garden is on the stove. I am my own Jewish Mother.

Speaking of chicken soup, I bought leeks to make another soup later. It is old-fashioned and very nice. Fry a leek or two in butter. Soak, then boil some pearl barley until tender. Mix both

~ 165 ~

with real chicken broth. Bring to the boil and add the juice of two lemons and serve at the table with yogurt. It is very fresh and good.

Two fat green bower birds are drinking from the bird-bath. Three white cockatoos flew screaming over, chasing a group of fleeing green parrots. 'Get out, this is our sky.' Who hasn't felt like a green parrot in their lifetime?

The Monet calendar Mr Waterlily gave me for Christmas has got, surprisingly, *Waterlilies circa 1903* for August. It is four years ago that I was in Monet's garden at Giverny looking at just those waterlilies with the white wisteria hanging in bunches. Now there was a gardener for you. The peonies big as hands, tall and in full bloom, grew among blue delphiniums, roses, poppies ... just a minute, let me run and get my album and I will tell you the names of the rest ... Yes, irises and foxgloves. And among all that, the pink house with its green shutters. Art just doesn't consist of making things on canvas, it is in living too.

How well those French painters understood that. Think of Vuillard; those interiors of his. It is his paintings of all the artists of the period that bring me close to tears. So much love. And Bonnard; the way he loved to paint women doing simple things. Holding a rose, about to put it in a vase. Women are at their most beautiful, these painters understood this so well, when they are preoccupied in work. Sewing, washing, cooking, reading. And men? I do not know. I never described one. I only write what they say and do. And often when men paint men, the *object* is being psychologically examined. I do not think it is so when women are painted by men. Except, perhaps, for Gertrude Stein. But, then, she *presented* herself as psychological. If they painted Alice, and I suppose they did, I expect it would be simply being, or at work. I must find out.

Think of the great self-portraits. Bonnard, Van Gogh, Rembrandt, Munch. Psychological studies all.

Time to put on some opera. The part in *Fidelio* where the prisoners come out of the dungeon is my favourite scene. I felt like that when I went to University as a mature age student.

I was going to lay down here one of my favourite poems; Auden's *Musée Des Beaux Arts* but I will keep that for later as I have found something that I think even he would say was greater and consoles me more today. The twenty-third Psalm.

The Lord is my shepherd; I shall not want.
He maketh me to lie down in green pastures: he leadeth me
*   beside the still waters.*
He restoreth my soul: he leadeth me in the paths of
*   righteousness for his name's sake.*
Yea, though I walk through the valley of the shadow of
*   death, I will fear no evil: for thou art with me; thy rod*
*   and thy staff they comfort me.*
Thou preparest a table before me in the presence of mine
*   enemies; thou anointest my head with oil; my cup runneth*
*   over.*
Surely goodness and mercy shall follow me all the days of
*   my life: and I will dwell in the house of the Lord forever.*

I think there has been nothing written before or since that I know of so comforting in a time of trouble.

Don't worry, I realise I may be sounding a little batty. Or I may even appear to be coming unhinged. If you'd had death threats, you'd be quoting the Psalms too.

I wanted so much to keep this a calm and soothing book, but I do not think any longer that I can.

It does not need a mind of too many neurones to figure out who is making these threats. We don't need to call Miss Marple either. David is getting me a view hole for my front door. Feeling rather foolish, I put the poker by the door telling myself I was behaving like a drama queen. But then, thinking of the scenes I witnessed in the city, I left it there. I'm a pacifist and also I'm here for a peaceful life. I want to learn to fly like a bird and live in the top of a beautiful tree.

Monday, 11 August
The violets are out. A small fairy field of them blooming like the answer to a humble prayer. The house smells of daphne. The scent always reminds me of being in hospital after I'd had my first baby. It is strangely not only a beautiful scent, but a

little bit antiseptic too. I hope they never think of putting that scent in washing-up detergent. It's bad enough they've almost ruined the lemon.

Last night in a half-sleep I wrote a poem about Giverny and today I typed it out. More redemption through work. I have two final interviews to do today and it should all be over. Then we wait for the critics to have their say.

Tuesday, 12 August
Sun's out and I am off to Adelaide. Green bower birds are drinking from the bird-bath. They seem such a thirsty bird. I am going to the post office to send off a manuscript to a publisher. Put things in envelopes, she says. Well, today it is a big thing in a big envelope.

I think about what a radio broadcaster with the ABC in Sydney said to me last week: 'You have to book a terrestial line.' I stared at him and asked him to repeat it so he did. Then I thought of what a physics student told me at the poetry workshop for Lithgow High School. He said the earth wasn't round as I'd just said, but, in fact, oval with the ends sheared off. 'The shape of the human eye, really,' he said laconically. Those three things mingle like a plait in my mind and I am waiting to write something about them. Sometimes, the word is simply *awe*.

Wednesday, 13 August
I am mad on planting. Today, through a kind of miracle, I planted two roses and at last, a white magnolia. The magnolia is called *Soulangiana Alba*. The tag says: 'deciduous, medium to tall shrub with white lily-like fragrant flowers before the leaves in Spring.' Who could ever resist these descriptions on plants standing like old sticks in nurseries? The roses are Golden Jubilee: 'Full blooming, fragrant, yellow tinged with pink.' And Garden Party: 'Delicate cream edged with pink.' All this, because, out of the blue, Martin Philips rang me to say he was here, staying at the Carrington with a friend. They came to coffee and off we went with Sarah who is staying with me because her house is still in danger from the pine trees, to the

local nursery which is my mecca. There, Martin bought me a flowering cherry tree. Called *Prunus Fugenzo*. 'Double deep pink blossom, bronze autumn foliage.' I have longed for a flowering cherry. That wet pink icing we walk through down the street in spring. The time David wore the floral hat straight out of *The Importance of Being Earnest*.

I put the magnolia just where Lydia put the stick so long ago when David trailed the hose in the curve that later I followed with bricks that was to be a garden bed. 'Here,' she said 'is where the magnolia goes.' And now, there it is.

After the visit to the nursery we came back here and had lunch of pasta, salad and wine. Then we walked from Olympian Rock to Lyrebird Dell and home through that magical horse-shoe-shaped trail.

Why, I ask myself, do I ever leave. Nothing bad ever happens to me here. It is only the city. But this is a very romantic notion. The fact is, here, alone, I would go mad with the isolation and the lack of intimacy. I have lots of friends, but I need intimacy. Yet here there is a healing quality. There is no doubt about it.

Sometimes I think of Graham Greene. He said something to the effect that there are only, in this life, victims and victors and one can only hope to be a victim. That sounds a queer thing to say on first reading, perhaps, but I think it is true. Who would want to be white just now in South Africa unless you were fighting on the side of justice for the black side? No, I don't see myself as a victim, but through a cunning undercurrent, a survivor. So, in a way, I want to make a dialectic from it and be neither a victim nor a victor. Simply one who came out on the other side. Into that land of health and justice. But that is not what he said.

I was thinking about what are some of the best things to do in life. Such a simple wild thought. Audacious too. I am certain Socrates did not think like this. But there are a few things that are particularly good and privileged to do. One is to bath a baby. Another, to light a fire to heat someone or oneself. To make love. To make love, actually, does that in the best circumstances. It is a curious thing but it seems so. Cooking, too, is good. Planting, planning perhaps, anything that might be beautiful or useful. Prayer, I think, now, since I saw nuns pray at some of the most horrible places on earth. And faith, above all, I think, faith. Without that we have no hope and without hope we cannot live. If I had a daughter now, I would call her Faith.

Thursday, 14 August
Still unable to live in her house because of tilting pines, Sarah just read out: 'Never lead against a hitter unless you can out-hit him.' That's a gem from Ernest Hemingway and she says it is meant for me to take as my present motto. And hers, she says, reading again from the Victoria Roberts satirical tea-towel is a Patrick White joke: 'If I have not lost my mind I can sometimes hear it preparing to defect.' She is understandably gloomy today. Wishes the pine would fall and she to be under it. It is a strange quiet grey day. Either you feel like yawning or the atmosphere feels ominous. I rode up the Mall, shopped and posted and settled myself in the centre of the energetic, domestic and that hearty part of life.

Friday, 15 August
Sun after rain. A good day for weeding. I didn't say I will weed, I just say it is a good day for for it. My compost heap is doing well now. Worms galore. I am quite keen on this heap. Funny how you can get ardent about the most unlikely things. Some can learn to love a rat. Tiny green birds flew into the garden this morning. Smaller than sparrows, they flew off waving. Hello, goodbye.

Today I dug three holes. A statement of intent. They are on the front so-called nature strip between the beech trees and the street. In these three holes I want three flowering cherry trees. White or pink. White, I think.

Philippa came and had afternoon tea and walked around the garden helping me decide where to plant the cherry Martin gave me.

Speaking of the best things one can do, here's Judah Waten on his idea about art:

For my part I am in love with the real world and I believe

this to be true of most fiction writers. My aim, using Conrad's words, 'is to make you see' and also to make a statement on life ... Art is not an autonomous act of the imagination; art extends our knowledge of life and helps liberate mankind by breaking down the barriers of ignorance.

That was a man well aware of, and dedicated to his politics. A real visionary.

And for my part, I am in love with art. I am not sure about the real world. My perception of it changes. I think art increases love. We only have art and love and they are all that can save us. Sometimes I doubt even they can, but I cling to them as they are all we have.

Saturday, 16 August
Cold, cold, cold. At Snaps Lydia gave me the Honeysuckle Cottage rose catalogue. The descriptions beggar belief for their romanticism. But in this case the romanticism is not dangerous. These are simply romantic plants.

Sunday, 17 August
To kill myself or not to kill myself. Deciding against it for the present, I planted the flowering cherry among the roses. It has taken several days of looking to find a place where it will grow without blocking other trees nor damaging the perspective of the view from the back room.

The tulips are up and among them, pansies struggling through. I weeded around some of them. Some hydrangeas in a vase in the bathroom were left there so long they sprouted. I have planted them in the front garden among some other hydrangeas under the Japanese maples.

Yesterday Mr Waterlily arrived. We walked to see the fallen snow gum. Later we sat by the fire and talked about the life we share. With death threats in the air like black, black birds, it is best I go away. Some time ago I was planning to go to Adelaide, but because I have no money, I had changed my mind. Now I will borrow it and go.

The first pink buds of prunus are bursting outside my bedroom window. Spring is coming, it is throbbing. I can hear it.

Thursday, 21 August
Adelaide, Adelaide, full of lovers Adelaide. Crows are calling, rabbits are running, rain is falling.

I am at Norton Summit with friends. There is a two-acre garden of native trees around this house and through these trees at dusk and early morning, rabbits run.

Above the valley and Morialta Falls, crows float and call as if lost in that interior dialogue no one else knows between man and wife. It is secret, it is unfathomable, and it is loud, open, unashamed, but deeply mysterious.

For twenty-three hours I sat in a bus that passed through a dozen small country towns with their sad and empty streets. Sad only to outsiders, as full of meaning and history to the inhabitants as the veins of their own hands.

Past hundreds of kilometres of saltbush plains where small floral carpets melt into each other to make a grand one. The driver put on films through these parts because of the lack of scenery, as he put it. Dashes of purple, lilac, pink, grey and white melted like running paint as we sped past.

At Broken Hill we passed the huge grey slag heaps left like the detritus of the mind of a man after a hard night out. Broken Hill feels earnest; full of the realities I know little of. And those I know of I flee from.

Saturday, 23 August
Wild white violets. I gathered a posy of them as I came in from lunch at the Wilkins. Thing of how you might smell after drinking the forbidden honey from the fields of Elyssium. It is a white and delicate holy scent. Even to sniff it makes you feel like an interloper. It is not for humans. We can only steal it.

I went to lunch at Philip and Marisa's home. After a few glasses of an Italian white wine, so delicate it looks like rain, a talk about our work, and then pasta which Philip ground out of a noisy machine while Philip Glass was playing on the record machine; this served with a sauce of artichokes, broad beans and a kid is something not easily forgotten. Then carpaccio, with a salad and a sauce of avocado oil, vinegar and garlic and brown and also white Italian bread. Enough said.

Outside the lemon tree bowed down with its yellow load and the rain wept as if at a destiny which we hoped was not ours.

Tuesday, 26 August
Yesterday a friend and I climbed the rough and rugged hills around Morialta Falls. Finally, trying to get over a grey rocky hill, we were driven back when the path ended and black-berries formed a shield like a beach in wartime covered with barbed wire. Yellow wattle is out waving everywhere. I try hard to understand why this landscape always has a morbid depressing quality to me. A wide-open flat landscape even if it has not a tree in sight never has this effect on me. It is open and exciting where the line of the horizon pings like a wire fence on a hot day. It is like a violin string stretched fine and hard. It longs to break.

I am in Norwood now at Connie and Angela's home. It is wet and the tall gum with the pale pink trunk outside this study waves two thin branches to the sky like a woman bearing a tray of leaves. The trunk is no longer pink, but pearly grey. I assume it turns pink in the spring or summer. Over the fish pond a thin white flowering broom waves like a low cloud. It is very Japanese.

Friday, 29 August
I have been to Sydney. It is a weird life. Barely enough money to feed myself, and yet flown to Sydney by ABC television to do an interview.

I sat on the old wooden table on the balcony at Balmoral where we did the poetry anthology for so many months. The day was bright and sunny with a sea breeze. In the background the sea came in and out as it ever does and I ate lunch with the interviewer and talked about the book. Then we went down to the small island linked by a Japanese bridge to the cream beach and with wind surfers behind me like butterflies, and the Heads forming two brackets with a hyphen of blue horizon between them, read my poem *Eve*.

I had dinner at Café Troppo with Mr Waterlily, shared a thousand kisses and smiles and some grilled octopus and was thoroughly happy. We went home and made the moon turn green with grief and envy while the stars fell fainting on their backs.

Then the early airport trip and back to Adelaide before lunch. As Ned Kelly said before they hanged him: 'Such is life.' Between the poverty and the riches, between the madness and the sanity, between the quiet the frenzy, between the ugliness, the beauty, between the hatred the love. Oh, I could put a white gardenia behind my ear and dance up the passage.

Sometimes life seems so intense and volatile it feels like sniffing ether. When I was younger it was like that almost all the time. I am quieter now, paler, more sober, but these moments do return and how I love them. If life is to be led I want it led at the finest pitch: tuned up, elegant, refined, intense with a longing such as the sandcastle has when it discovers it can never ever become a hill.

I keep thinking about the landscape here in the Adelaide Hills. It has a strange effect on me. As if it has dragged a claw through my mind. It disturbs me and I can never understand why. It is so melancholy and so desolate. Yet truly desolate places don't affect me the way those gums and spare bare paddocks do. It is as if they are mourning and I join in too. Even as a child at Gawler it affected me the same way. I walked through it full of despair. Yet, for the first twelve years of my life, reared in a little fishing town on the edge of a desert facing all that space I never felt like that. In front and behind. Man is simply a stick in the landscape in Australia. Painters draw two lines; one a horizontal, the other a smaller vertical. There it is. Man in the landscape. Perhaps it is that faced with these trees the space is lost and the beginning of the panic of imprisonment begins.

~13~

September

Tuesday, 2 September

Happy Spring! Post-modernist, post-object art. Who can say the day it was invented? Was it when Paul Valery one day in the Shakespeare and Company Bookshop in Paris took a pen and drew on the exposed knee of Cyprian Miss Beach, a face she wished never to erase? Or was it during the Roman Empire when a Roman Empress lay down on a stage, covered herself with honey and asked men to lick it from her? Things are invented more by a name than an act, if you ask me.

I have been thinking about this because I am reading a ravishing book, *Sylvia Beach and the Lost Generation* by Noel Riley Fitch. I can't get enough of it and am eating it like an apple.

Yesterday full of dread I caught the train to Gawler to see my mother. I wished to see my mother but not to make the journey. I hate, hate, hate those plains with small houses, bare front lawns and a fate hanging over them I fled when I was seventeen. Not that I ever lived in a house like that. My mother made a secret nest wherever she was and filled it with flowers and beautiful furniture, delicious food, wood fires and early nights. The night before the visit I kept waking up with that feeling of grey panic as if you're about to faint. Breaking out in a sweat as if you're poisoned, you know as the needle goes in before an operation, there is no escape.

It is such a luxury to read. As I said, ever since I had a dose of post-partum depression after my son was born, I have hardly been able to read anything except the few things that totally seduce me. I walked into a ward full of women who, like me, had just given birth. They were reading magazines and looked quite cheerful and normal. I went back to my room and got into the bed and knew I could no longer even act normal. Ever since that time I have only been able to read a few things. Before I had had the baby I read everything that came my way.

On our farm, reading was not encouraged. As a result, I read like a criminal. To this day, I feel guilty, although now grateful, when I read. For all the theories about education I still think there is something to be recommended in keeping things as secret vices. Who would eat spinach if made to and roused on and told one must and not be allowed leave the table until one had? Talk about a killer of all lust, greed or passion. Who, in the end, would make love if told one must at this time and even, dare I say it, in front of others and for approval and because it was good for one. No, it's best left as a private vice, all these things should be natural, secret and forbidden. Or is it that I have the true nature of a criminal? Perhaps.

Speaking of post-object art, I suppose the final definition of a great meal is just that. On Sunday friends gave lunch for ten at their home. I left at six o'clock and even so the pudding was still to come. I will tell you the menu because it interested me.

First, grissini made with a yeast mixture in their pasta machine. These were served with a dish of pickled capsicum, onion, carrot and cauliflower, sprinkled with fresh mint and dried chillies. Then, because I asked specially, a lemon salad. All that was served with pernod or champagne. I kept wanting to eat more of the lemon salad but reminded myself lemon and salt combine to make an emetic. Then a homemade pasta of a kind thick as your little finger with a cooked fennel sauce. I was not keen on that. Then small soufflés of smoked barramundi set in the middle of big white plates with a dash of horseradish mixed with beetroot, a spoon of mayonnaise, a spoon of hazelnut butter and a leaf of small raddichio, and a leaf or two of other Italian herbs whose names I don't know. It looked like a painting. Everything laid out separately with an inch or so between. Then an hour or so later came two legs of kid marinated in milk and juniper berries for a couple of days. These were boiled in the marinade after searing in oil and butter and then finished off roasted briefly in the oven. An orange and whitlof and olive salad and a mixed green salad and bread came with this. Afterwards an assortment of Italian cheeses.

Bottles of red wine were passing around and I took some of all. By this time it was dusk and I left riding the bike particularly straight with concentration.

Wednesday, 10 September
Horses fall and rise like fortunes. At the Murray Bridge picnic races, I stood by the railing and watched horses stream past with jockeys like melted rainbows on their backs. The thunder of their feet, the curses of their riders and closer to the rail I press and this is the thing I love; the power and terror best next to death. Flying or drowning in your love.

On the other hand, outside this room the white broom hangs like a white brush stroke over the pond, contemplating only the quiet air and the peace of a Zen memory. Yin and Yang. Yin and Yang.

I have had a proposal. The old-fashioned sort that men used to make to women. But wait for it, it's from a married man. I haven't replied. But I am startled. I could come unhorsed over this. Lie like one of the jockeys I saw in orange silk on the green turf holding my leg and groaning as the ambulance pulls up. Or worse, lie still like the other jockey bent with his shiny boots flopped down like a doll. Or, I suppose, in the best of all possible worlds, I could flash past not using a whip racing on among the fast bunch running to the post in the happy thunder of our feet.

I will tell you about our picnic. The Wilkins invited me, and each guest brought a course for the menu. It began under a big gum tree at tables we set up with chairs and an old white linen starched cloth. Greek appetisers and pitta bread with champagne. God how these Adelaidians live. Then later we had a cold omelette called frittata made with spinach and sorrel. That was eaten like slices of cake in our fingers. Then carpaccio with green virgin olive oil and small thin squares of mozarella cheese.

The salad was small leaves of sorrel and others I don't know. A Sicilian salad too, of cooked celery, onion and eggplant tossed in vinegar, sugar and tomato paste with green olives and capers in it. It's queer and nice. The apple and cinnamon cake I made was flat but they very politely ate it and called it tasty. By this time it was four o'clock and money lost, coffee drunk, clouds coming over, we packed and drove home. Not at all unhappy.

Coming down the Adelaide hills the sea spread out like a bolt of shot taffeta under a red liquid sun sinking, drowning in it like Icarus.

I keep thinking of Judith Rodrigues' poem *How Do You Know It's The Right One?*

> *Can you play it on a keyboard?*
> *On one string?*
> *Is it partial to silence?*
>
> *Can you exalt it*
> *continuously?*
> *Can you debase it?*
>
> *Can you look at it curdled*
> *and pasty*
> *in the glass after midnight?*
>
> *And eat it and drink it*
> *whatever –*
> *it with its memories*
>
> *and malaise, years and days of it?*
> *Must you have it?*
> *Will you love it or live with it?*

Friday, 12 September
It's raining here in Adelaide and I am writing poems. When all else fails, write, I say, write.

Yesterday an old friend, John Robson, drove me to Gawler to visit my Father's grave. I had never seen it. It was twenty-one years ago plus one day that he died. I have spent twenty-one years pretending to myself in my darkest heart that I was his widow. If I couldn't be the wife, I could at least become the widow. Together we knelt and weeded the grave where the grey gravel is growing thinner. I put some white and yellow daisies that my Mother gave me beside the grey granite headstone. It has just his name and death date on it. Nothing else. A strange and reticent rough hewn headstone, rather like himself. I said: 'Deserter,' as I walked away, got in the car and drove down the winding road.

We found a spot facing long green paddocks. We opened up the wine and sandwiches and ate and talked and all the while I was quite dry-eyed. The fact is I am bitter. In beside him is where I always wished to be. I could manage while he was still around and ever since he left, things fall apart like dolls worn out from love. I could never stitch or hold any parts together. I kept dancing, smiling, trying to look normal. I'm told the phrase is pathological grief. It is a name but it doesn't help at all.

In the meantime I got jilted. Never believe a married man in love, my dears. It is as foolish as to listen to chickens cackling and believe they are reading from the Bible. My heart's not broken. I am merely sighing. He changed his mind a mere eight hours after I said 'Yes'. Is it panic, cowardice or just a vicious game? I no longer care or know. He'll hold a torch until he's dead and I will proceed with living. It's four years now since he first jilted me ... I think it must be my fault. I lose my brains when I see love coming round the corner on its old black motorbike. Off it gets, undoes its helmet and I stand there hypnotised, hopeless, foolish, dangerous and helpless. Later on when he kicks the motor, climbs on and rides away, I come to my senses, shake my head, the dazed look fades and once more I am rational, resigned and at peace. But not a jot the wiser.

Wednesday, 17 September
Home.

Daffodils are waving in the wind and beside them the dark blue grape hyacinths sit like rich fruit. The yellow of the daffodil is exactly the measure of the blue of the grape hyacinths.

The prunus is out and when I walked round to the Denisons to collect my mail I saw their big tree with the pink petals covering the lawn just as it did this time last year. In a week or so the flowering cherries will be out. And then this will all be over. A year will have passed.

Sarah drove down to meet the train this morning when I got

off at Leura. The wind was cold and wild and kerosene heaters were burning in the store where I went to get supplies. I lit the fire and told Sarah my news while we drank tea. Sarah has sold her house. She is moving to the beach. The mountains, as David said, are not for everyone.

There is a rich pink camellia bigger than the saucer here on this table. The pots of camellias on the verandah are in full bloom. I picked hellebore and daffodils and there are glass jugs of them around. Also some daphne beside my bed.

I have been out doing matron's round in the garden. The white hyacinths are out like white thighs. Pansies are blooming too and even the roses have plenty of leaves and so far no aphids. The pink clematis I planted at the back steps is full of growth and leaves and I cannot wait to see that dusky pink flower.

Yesterday I arrived back in Sydney at seven in the morning on a bus. Mr Waterlily met me and drove me home to Leichhardt. Since then I have barely been able to stay awake. I have a dose of bus lag.

Connie and Angela arrived home from New York on Sunday and Connie's son and I drove to the airport at Adelaide to meet them. Full of shrieks and cries the cases were undone and our presents opened. I have Diorama perfume and a bag painted in a reproduction of a Matisse painting. It is hanging on a pink cord above this kitchen bench. Connie and Angela were tear-gassed at the opening night of the Metropolitan in New York. A terrorist threw a tear-gas bomb so all fled. Now that is the only exception, I think, to my rule to eschew almost everything of the twentieth century in this story. I could not resist that snippet. But if you do not like it, put it aside and pretend you did not read it. You too, can cancel what you do not like in this game. The fact is the reader always has more power than the writer. But they don't often realise it. With books, it takes two to tango.

I am feeling a bit gloomy. It's not that I am all that hurt over being jilted second time around; more resigned than anything I suppose. But what one needs to realise is that the very door you worked so hard to open in your desperate attempt to escape only, in fact, leads to another cell and so on and so forth, right down the block. It is death row we are all on and there is no escaping from that. I have been realising that to be a married man's mistress is to be the ugly sister that had to be given away. The one who wasn't sold when the sale was on. All relationships are power struggles and this world goes round on trade. Trade and trade-offs.

I am also rather anxious. All this could upset my apple-cart and these here apples are all I have. And I still hope to be happy but the signs at the moment, my gypsy sweetheart, are not good.

Yet Mr America, or Lt Pinkerton, if you prefer, is coming here to visit me and to stay a few days. We make love like people the night before their hanging. It is dangerous. It is ill advised. Too precipitous. Not a wise thing at all. But then I always said I would never have a broken-backed old nag but would ride a wild white horse or none at all. So be it.

And the worrying thing about all this is that I have only a few more pages to get it right. 'Is there an end to this plot? That end could not be ethical since ethics is an intervention of men, not of inscrutible Gods.' Jorge Luis Borges.

As I lay on my white bed this afternoon thinking all this over I thought I heard the snap of this book closing with disapproving sighs, no, not from men but from women. Phyllis Chessler says in her book *Women and Madness* that 'women are still in the harem. When a woman tries to escape, it is not a man who grips her at the gate but a woman. It is a woman who pulls her back by the hair of her head'. Men never do their own dirty work. They don't need to. They have arranged it so that the women do it for them. It is called God's Police. In Adelaide I had a goodly dose of it. How I loathe those who take the moral high ground.

Enough of all this. I am baking a pink shiny trout in butter and foil that Mr Waterlily got yesterday from the fish markets in Pyrmont. Take some courage with each bite, madam, and get a grip on yourself. These complaints do not become you and only bore the reader. They spread the anxiety like butter on a hot potato and serve little purpose. My telephone is cut off and that makes me feel alone. Don't think too badly of me. I said that also to a friend when we said goodbye in Adelaide. I didn't realise it at the time, but it's a quote.

Thursday, 18 September
George came shortly after I had found some money left here for me by friends who came to stay while I was away. They played bridge night and day for two days. Together George and I raced over to the nursery and there I got the three flowering cherries I had dug the holes for before I went away. I got some blue violas too and have been out on my hands and knees planting them. George bought a white Alba magnolia and a flowering cherry. When he gets his tax return, he is going to run over in his car and spend a thousand dollars at the nursery, he says.

My telephone is now reconnected and I feel much calmer. It is not so easy living alone without a telephone. In the night even if I couldn't find the number of the Katoomba police in any panic, I would at least feel safer knowing I could try. I had to ring seven times to get it reconnected though I paid the bill two weeks ago. In the end I said I would consider hanging myself if I did not get it back on today. I rode home from the post office and lo! the phone was working. The manager from Penrith rang and apologised and said they did not want blood on their hands. So, in the cottonwool of bureaucracy, human cries, if they are wild or mad enough, sometimes get through.

Somehow, those three holes dug with faith seem an omen to me now. If I can get the trees for those holes I can accomplish plenty else too.

I am reminded of the story my Mother told me about the time I went with my German grandmother to the Tumby Bay show. After buying a kewpie doll with some money I had been given, I walked round the oval then back to the man selling the dolls, and said I didn't like that one any longer and would like another one. He let me give it back and take another. Grandmother said to my Mother that with nerve like that I would go far. So here I am still asking for another kewpie doll.

There are white buds on the apple tree outside the kitchen window. And pink on the peach. The foxgloves have big stalks leaping up. The tulips have buds thrusting too. A pink hyacinth on the bench scents this whole room. So what if the man I loved and would again, won't live with me. Is this sour grapes? Possibly. But for whatever reason, today I have a respite from longing. After all, let's face it, what is a human being but a bag of longing.

Friday, 19 September
The nurseryman delivered the trees. Now they are in their beds, all lined up just how matron likes. I bought a good plain white pot yesterday too and in that now sits a Debutante pink camellia I repotted. The small daphne is in a turquoise green china pot and for once I have done as I was told. Edna Walling advises that many shrubs, daphne in particular, don't like to be repotted into very large pots until they too are large. So the small daphne now sits at the front door in a small pot.

I strewed a whole big bag of fertiliser around and hosed it in on all the roses and azaleas, trees and annuals too. I feel as smug as if I had just given my baby a big bottle of pepped up milk and now it lies smiling in its sleep, satisfied and full of promise of long limbs, strong bones and so on. Well, a few blooms will do in this case.

Saturday, 20 September
Sunny day at Leura. The sun pours down like honey from an urn overturned. My halo glows. I have been weeding. One hand has stigmata on it as David pointed out at Snaps. It is not from sanctity; merely weeding with a trowel.

Birds are calling, a flute concerto is playing and I am lonely but not dissatisfied. Can I accept my lot? It is a lot and I must accept, it is all I will get. I remind myself that if this was snatched from me, as it could so easily be, how I would long and pine for it. These sticks that I dream will be a garden, this peace, this freedom, the walks I could take if I went out of my gate, the typewriter waiting. I've even got some stamps and that is not to be sneezed at. *Seize the Day* writes Saul Bellow. Well, I might as well, no good sitting waiting for something better to mosey along. This is it. The present is all one has, but how to squash the longing. That's the trick. A sense of awe might help. Here's a quote from *Seize the Day*:

> 'In telling you this,' said Tamkin with one of his hypnotic subtleties, 'I do have a motive. I want you to see how some people free themselves from morbid guilt feelings and follow their instincts. Innately, the female knows how to cripple by sickening a man with guilt. It is a very special destruct, and she sends her curse to make a fellow impotent. As if she says, "Unless I allow it, you will never more be a man". But men like my old Dad and Mr Rappaport answer, "Woman, what art thou to me?" You can't do that yet. You're a halfway case. You want to follow your instincts, but you're worried still.'

The white clematis I planted at the front verandah post, that fainted limp as a dying Saviour against the post, has resurrected itself. It is covered in leaves and vigorous. I almost pulled it out thinking it was dead.

Sunday, 21 September
I have been out planting ground covers around the new cherries. I simply love writing sentences like that.

I rode the bike down the street with Spring running its fingers through my hair and not a worry in the world disturbed me except the thought of how soon I could plant the ground covers Philippa brought me yesterday. Like a gambler longing to get into the casino.

I am making buttermilk scones and fruit cakes with pecan nuts in them. The cakes are to send to friends in Adelaide to thank them. No doubt the wretched postage will break the bank. For such a practical person I am oddly impractical: as has been remarked before.

I have been out squashing aphids. Last night reading some 1970 *Australian Garden* magazines I got from the St Vincent de Paul shop in Katoomba, I found a recipe for an aphid deterrent. This saves trying to grow the onions round the roses at which I was singularly unsuccessful last year. Here it is: Cut one pound of onions into small pieces. Pour boiling water on them and allow to stand for about ten hours. Add cold water to make two gallons. Water the plants first and then apply the onion water, a jam tin (one pound) to each plant. It is said it is not the smell that drives away the aphids but some property in the onions that gives to plants their own resistance to the pest.

I want some petunias and some love from a faithful man. I know where to buy the petunias.

It is uncomfortable to admit that I have not found what I wanted. Perhaps I would not have liked it if I had found it; but I would like to have found it, just to know. However, instead I choose men of whom I can only say: so steeped in duplicity was he, that he could not stand naked in the light of day and cast a shadow. Oh well, so what. Shrug, shrug.

I have hurt my back digging. It plucks at the strings behind my eyeballs. This back is sending up gloomy thoughts like bubbles.

Monday, 22 September
I've got the manure! Oh happy day. George came here and together we went to the stables. He did the work while I merely held the empty bags. Now as soon as my back will let me, I shall be seen spreading this holy compost around anything that might like it. Speaking of this back, George had to lift me from the floor where I was crawling backwards beside the fire this morning because I simply could not stand up after lighting it. But strangely, after two visitors came to afternoon tea I was suddenly better.

Penguin rang to say they have sold out of our book after only six weeks and are planning to reprint it at once.

One of the visitors arrived with a box in her arms containing a miniature country show. Apple and plum blossom, pickled green figs, medlar jelly, spring flowers: freezias, azaleas, lavender, forget-me-not, primula, phlox and English daisies. All this stood on the bench with a bunch of fresh herbs tied with a rubber band. We talked and drank tea until six o'clock. These two women are authors and speak about international publishers as if they were the local grocer.

Tuesday, 23 September
I have been out picking daffodils and grape hyacinths to take to town. It is so sunny and peaceful you can hear the birds fly. Here

I go to catch the train to dine with Mr Grumpy Waterlily. Wish me luck as you wave me goodbye. And, if his girlfriend again threatens to kill me, so be it. At least it would make my work suddenly sell.

Friday, 26 September
That Viking Eric has returned. There he was when I got home today, sitting up in his bed waving and blazing away. So now that is the first of the tulips and about twenty more to come.

I have been out spreading horse manure. Four bags have gone on and already the garden looks more cared for. I have such energy it is running through me like a river. Is it the Spring I wonder. I wilt a bit in winter and have a theory that the sun on my head starts up some deep boiler room inside and chug, chug, I start to churn and rush and work and to feel so well I could fight a tiger.

I have only a few pages or days to go to get this right. Yesterday I asked one of my visitors what she thought might end this Journal fittingly. She has written so many books and has taste and style I admire. She said if it can't be solved, this life, that is, and as life is never solved until it is over, perhaps, dot dot dot ... that was her suggestion. Do you like that? I do.

Yesterday I walked around the Rocks area in Sydney with Mr Waterlily and had lunch in the Lord Nelson Hotel, an early eighteenth-century sandstone three-storey colonial building. Before that I walked through Holy Trinity Church nearby. It has very good stained glass; the earliest is 1865. It's also called The Garrison Church.

There was an orchid show in the Town Hall and I walked through that too. An old man told me the secret of feeding orchids is to use fish emulsion once a fortnight alternating with Aquasol. He said to use only half what the label advises. So, orchid in the sunroom drooping and neglected and unfertile as the sad affair from which you came, help is coming. Big lush fronds of pink orchids may soon be mine.

At Mosman I had lunch with Peri in her garden. Under big straw hats we sat eating delicious cold food with the orange marmalade cat asleep at our feet on the green lawn. The next day we went for a walk round the Harbour looking at the gardens and the vast amounts of love some people have lavished on their most opulent plots. Everything grows down there as if it's Eden and God wants those two to be very, very sad about their eviction. It just blazes with colour. After the walk we had coffee at a restaurant with an old tiled pink floor, dark green walls and polished wood and brass bars and tables. Overhead wooden fans keep it cool and there, at any hour, you can sit back in a cane chair, order gin and tonic or iced coffees and think that any minute Somerset Maugham may walk in and begin taking notes. I felt so happy and intense sitting there with Peri and I said to her: 'I could go up in flame.'

On the bus going back to Leichhardt a young man got on with a big furled white flag about four metres long. Behind him came a young very blonde girl with a vast black plastic flag furled. It was Caroline. She laughed and sat down beside me and said, 'Hello Mum!' They had been to a student demonstration about university fees. When I haven't seen her for a while I get a shock to see how fair she is. It is as though her head is carved from a piece of white marble. I stare and stare at it, my eyes can't get enough of her. Now, while the sun is still out I am off to paint the back double doors a glossy white. They are red and I do not think it at all suitable.

Here's another fact. A delicious fact. Italians dry tomatoes in the sun. I am planning to do this in a week or two when we are certain of long successions of sunny days. Here's the way it's done. Cut red ripe tomatoes in halves and cover with salt. Dry in the sun. Bring in at night if cool or damp. It takes four or five days in hot sun. Dip them then in boiling water. Dry again in the sun. Pack into jars with garlic, olive oil and oregano. They are good as part of antipasto or with mozarella cheese and many other things too. You slice them and dress in olive oil.

It is dusk and standing at the back glass doors I gloated over my garden so bare to the eye of most, but to me, entirely beautiful. As I said to George last week, it is positively Churchillian this garden. Never has so much fuss been made over so little. All that is there at the moment are some sticks, some daffodils, some curved beds of roses just beginning to put out leaves and tall bare trees. But to me, none of this is of account. I see great white dove bracts on the handkerchief tree, the dogwood wild and big and blooming about twenty feet high. The roses covered in their yellow, white or pink flowers, the cherry spreading wide burdened down with blossom. The white garden, a mass of azaleas, ground covers and gardenias. The pansies turning a thousand faces to me and the petunias (not yet bought) full of bright colour sending out their scent on the dusk air. And there, too, in my mind, is the hammock swinging gently with my son asleep in the dappled light with his eyelids that particular translucent sheen he still has, and had in the photos I took of him, eyes closed smiling into the sun, in his bassinette. The petals of his toes fluttered on the edge of the cradle. And over the back steps and the decking burst huge yellow peace roses mingling with the blue clematis, the colour of the Virgin's gown. At one end climbs the dusky rose-pink clematis above the tan and yellow iris blooming next to one that is yellow, laced with blue. Beside these are the white carnations that came from cuttings from those Mr Waterlily sent to say something he could not say otherwise. Behind all this, the pink-trunked gums wave forty feet high in the air and my pergola stands weighed down with jasmine and blue wisteria in great bunches over which the bees quietly buzz before going off to the hive I have yet to get, from where I pour out honey into jars for friends to take home to the city. And so on.

Suddenly, unexpectedly, my Mother arrives with a friend in a taxi. She has two buckets of flowers in her hands and as she walks down the drive they slurp and scatter edelweiss. A drift of edelweiss. This, because I have seen her do it many times. Her friend is younger than she and is here to help my Mother on the journey. My daughter is sitting languidly in the wooden gazebo trailing a white arm over the open side and when she sees her grandmother, she leaps up and runs calling 'Muttee!' She flings herself on my Mother who puts down her buckets laughing, and, looking over Caroline's shoulder says: 'Hello, aren't you surprised?' She does not tell me there is a spot on my blouse; but instead says: 'That rigout suits you.' Hugh, hearing all this, turns round, sees and rolls out of the hammock and walks up the drive to take the buckets and the case my Mother's friend is carrying. I go inside to put the kettle on. Caroline takes Muttee by the hand and shows her the gazebo where they sit talking with the friend. Hugh comes inside to help me and says: 'Well, isn't this a surprise? Where will Muttee sleep?' I say: 'Thank God I've just had the study painted; I will make up the bed in there. I think she will like it. It was lucky you hung the new curtains for me. She will be comfortable in there.' I walk out with the tray smiling in the sun. And here endeth episode one thousand and twenty of *Blue Hills* on ABC radio and now you can all go back to work on the farm.

Saturday, 27 September
At Snaps this morning Lydia and David gave me a present of a big cake tin and some cooking scales. This because I often borrow theirs and they knew I needed these things. I have just made a chocolate cake with a third of a kilo of cooking chocolate chopped into pieces mixed with a rich chocolate cake mixture. It is swooning with richness and oozing with luxury. I made brownies too.

Peri is here. We sat at the small table down by the hammock with a magpie trying to take our spinach tart with salad. Later Peri sat embroidering with her back to the house, a yellow straw hat perched on her head, her hair ribbon moving on her neck, a lovely restful pose. I went inside and had a sleep.

I have found another thing to do with sundried tomatoes. It is called Tomato Gougére. Boil together 150 ml water with 60 grams unsalted butter. Off the flame add 90 grams of plain flour and mix in well. Beat in 1 egg and 1 egg yolk. Add 69 grams of gruyere cheese and 2 big tablespoons finely chopped sundried tomatoes. Place rounded tablespoons full of this dough in a circle on a lightly oiled baking tray. Continue until all the dough is used. The circle should be about 20 cm wide. Bake in a preheated 200°C oven for 35 minutes. Serve hot. This a Lee Bailey recipe. He is an American cookery writer who says one should not cook anything one does not like to eat. I cook almost nothing I do like to eat. The sun is pouring down, there is an opera on the radio and a bird is calling, calling outside this open window. Peri is reading and there is not much wrong with my world, as far as I know, right now.

Lt Pinkerton rang from Adelaide and is arriving for a week in Eden with me in ten days' time. I am not sure we are doing a wise thing. I will tell you why. Four years ago he left Sydney airport to go home to his job and to his wife. I went to Europe. It took a long time to recover and to relish this world properly again. But I managed it. I was determined not to have an affair on paper and live the rest of my life in the robbery of pining and longing with wistful looks at every sunset I saw. No. I wanted to face the sunset with nothing between us. Finally I managed it. It was in Vienna and there was a desecrated nineteenth-century Jewish cemetry, where the Nazis had opened the graves. Here I laid this love to rest. It was a very sad and green and beautiful place. Tall trees and ivy climbing over the upturned tombstones and around the empty family vaults. Because that American was Jewish it seemed appropriate several days later when I realised I had left the affair in that green sad place. And so now, I do not want to spit on the past, but to leave it alone. I have it as a relic and it is very important to me that we do not desecrate it or do anything to harm it. Yet here I am agreeing to all this. Who can chart the path of the human heart?

Sunday, 28 September
Mist is swirling round the house. Last night after dinner I read some of the poems in the Penguin anthology to Peri as she sat quietly stitching blue flowers. I have read her Ania Walwicz' *Australia* and also her *Daredevil*. Then I read my absolute favourite poem from the book – Margaret Scott's *Grandchild*. The hackles rise on my head as I read it. It is a truly ravishing poem about a very sentimental subject brilliantly and originally managed. I love it. It is a masterpiece. We played some opera records, drank the French champagne Peri brought with her, lit the candles and ate dinner.

Philippa is coming to morning tea and is bringing me some nasturtium plants. The black frost we had in August killed all the nasturtiums as well as a lot of native trees. The sap froze in their veins. Whose wouldn't if you saw a black frost coming and

~ 190 ~

you naked and alone? I lost my small red flowering gum that Guida gave me. Dead as a dodo. Perished.

Monday, 29 September
Our last day. The sparrows are pecking at the pink tips of blossoms on the apple tree. It is a year now, a full circle. Full in many senses. I dreamt last night it was raining horse manure. I ran round with my wheelbarrow and spade. That must be a good omen. Perhaps Jung would say a feeling of opulence and good fortune and great optimism. It seems so to me.

Peri has gone home. We went to a French restaurant for lunch yesterday and while she had garlic brains and spatchcock in citrus and honey, I had mussels with parsley, wine and cream mopped up with bread.

We played 'What five foods would you take to a desert island for three months to live and keep well with only heating and water available to cook them'. She choose coconuts, oranges, fish, bread and tomatoes. I chose potatoes, cabbage, fish, bread and tea.

Then it continued with what five people would you take and what five books. We decided to take each other, naturally, or was it out of politeness she said that? Then not to take men because we simply thought it would work better: perhaps because there would not be the threat of a split camp or other problems. Peri chose the Bible because she hasn't read it. I chose the complete works of Shakespeare, and the complete works of Emily Dickinson. (You must have a poet you can re-read often and see more levels and not get bored.) I said I would invite Angela because she'd be fun and would keep her head in times of trouble. By this time Peri was chosing a vacherin with strawberries, and I was drinking the last of the wine, so we stopped. You can complete the list if you wish. Come with us.

It's evening now and George and I have been to the nursery to get a satsuma plum for his garden and petunias and delphiniums. It is raining and a perfect day for planting. I warned George it was useless to plant petunias without laying out snail-killer. I could see as a Buddhist he did not like this at all; but he said nothing. They will just be stubs in the morning like a cheque book unless those blue pellets are around.

I am going on here in the most normal way I can, while in my heart I have that feeling you get before you part. Some one is going a long way away. I want to pack you a tin of biscuits and give you a fond farewell, pushing into your arms as you climb the gangplank, bunches of white cherry blossom, armsful of daffodils; ah, I do not like farewells.

When you get into your cabin as you must now very shortly, if you ask yourself was she happy, as she was determined to be when she came to live in the mountains, answer 'yes' and 'no'. More 'yes' than 'no'.

I have been out planting petunias. Two punnets of white, two of blue and two of many colours. I did it in the rain so they lie moist and blinking in their new beds hardly, I hope, aware of what has happened. Beside me I have hung by this table the cross-stitched sampler Peri gave me. The legend reads:

Tis a heavenly
pleasure indeed,
curbing passion's
wild excess;
And when I
do not succeed
Tis a pleasure
none the less.

Perhaps I should have it carved in marble and leave it for my epitaph.

And now, without delay, I want you to walk up the gangplank, not looking back and take with you my love.